Official Guide to the

Wales Coast Path: **North Wales Coast**

Chester to Bangor

View to the Great Orme and West Shore, Llandudno

Llwybr Arfordir Cymru
Wales Coast Path

Official Guide to the

Wales Coast Path
North Wales Coast

Chester to Bangor

80 miles/ 125 kilometres of
superb coastal walking

Lorna Jenner

Alyn Books
www.alynbooks.co.uk

Text: Lorna Jenner

Series editor: Tony Bowerman

Introductory section: Tony Bowerman and Lorna Jenner

Photographs: © Crown copyright (2014) Visit Wales, Shutterstock, Dreamstime, Carl Rogers, Lorna Jenner, Glyn Jones, Carole Johnson, Jo Danson, Jackie Lewis, Steve Young, John Power, Mike Ellis, John Coppack, Pat Gore, Tony Trasmundi, Siobhan Raw, Karen Hodgkinson, Mike Taylor, Adrian Pink, Daily Post, John Dixon, Flintshire County Council, Ruth Thomas, Geoff Pickard

Design: Carl Rogers

© Crown copyright 2014. All rights reserved.
Licence number 100022856

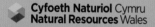
Cyfoeth Naturiol Cymru
Natural Resources Wales

Series created by **Northern Eye Books**
Published by: **Alyn Books** under licence

ISBN **978-0-955962-51-6**

A CIP catalogue record for this book is available from the British Library

www.alynbooks.co.uk
www.walescoastpath.co.uk
www.northerneyebooks.co.uk
www.top10walks.co.uk

Acknowledgements: Warm thanks are due to everyone who helped make this book a reality. Thank you, in particular, to Natural Resources Wales who have worked on on the Wales Coast Path since 2007 and have been generous with their friendly advice and support. Thanks also to the Wales Coast Path officers for each local authority along the path, Wales on View picture researchers, freelance photographers, local historians and everyone else who has played a part.

First published in 2015 by:

Alyn Books
Cilcain, Flintshire CH7 5PD

info@alynbooks.co.uk

For trade and sales enquiries, please call
01928 723 744 or 01352 741676

Twitter: @WalesCoastUK
@Alynbooks

Contents

Wales Coast Path: Discover the shape of a nation 6

Wales Coast Path: An 870-mile coastal adventure 8

The Best of the North Wales coast 28

North Wales Coast: Part of the Wales Coast Path 30

Walking the North Wales coast - map and distance chart 32

Day Sections 35

Limited for time? the North Wales Coast in a nutshell 40

A brief history of the North Wales Coast 42

Wildlife on the North Wales Coast 50

Waders, terns and wild goats 52

The North Wales Coast section of the Wales Coast Path 58

Day Section 1: Chester to Flint 60

A birdwatcher's paradise 69

Docks and shipyards 70

Day Section 2: Flint to Talacre 72

A military stronghold 75

Day Section 3: Talacre to Pensarn 88

Sand dune sanctuary 95

Day Section 4: Pensarn to Llandudno 98

Sun and sand 102

Day Section 5: Llandudno to Conwy 110

Birds and butterflies 117

A hilltop stronghold 121

Day Section 6a: Conwy to Llanfairfechan Coastal Route 124

Castles and conquest 130

The road to Ireland 136

Day Section 6b: Conwy to Llanfairfechan Upland Route 138

Shipwrecks and gales 150

Day Section 7: Llanfairfechan to Bangor 152

Useful Information

Welsh Coastal Place Names 162

Visitor Information 164

Wales Coast Path Official Guides 167

Official Guides to the Wales Coast Path

The Official Guides to the Wales Coast Path are the only ones endorsed by **Natural Resources Wales**, the body responsible for co-ordinating the development of the route. The Official Guides split the Path into seven main sections with a guide for each. Together, they cover the entire 870-mile Path from the outskirts of Chester in the north to Chepstow in the south.

For details of the full range of Official Guides to the Wales Coast Path, see:

www.walescoastpath.gov.uk/plan-your-trip/guidebooks.aspx

Wales Coast Path
Discover the shape of a nation

Wales is the largest country in the world with a continuous path around its entire coast. The **Wales Coast Path** promises 870 miles/1400 kilometres of unbroken coastal walking, from the outskirts of Chester in the north to Chepstow in the south. Along the way you'll experience the very best of Wales: stunning scenery, stirring history, Welsh culture, and wildlife in abundance. If you tackle only one big walk in your life, make it this one. It's unmissable.

Conwy Mountain, North Wales

South Stack Lighthouse, Anglesey

Puffin

Caernarfon Castle

Ynyslas dunes, Gwynedd

Bottlenose dolphins

Tenby, Pembrokeshire

Rhossili Bay, Gower

Nash Point, Glamorgan Heritage Coast

IR IN THESE STO
DR·HORIZO
AIS·AWENS

Millennium Centre, Cardiff

Wales Coast Path
An 870-mile coastal adventure

When the **Wales Coast Path** opened in May 2012, Wales became the largest country in the world with a continuous path around its entire coast. Walkers can now enjoy unparalleled coastal walking around the Welsh seaboard from top to bottom: from the outskirts of the ancient walled city of Chester, on the Dee Estuary in the north, to the pretty market town of Chepstow, on the Severn Estuary, in the southeast.

The official, signposted and waymarked path covers roughly 870 miles/1400 kilometres and starts and finishes close to the ends of the historic 177 mile/285 kilometre Offa's Dyke National Trail. This means keen walkers can make a complete circumnavigation of Wales; a total distance of around 1,050 miles/1,685 kilometres. Ever keen for a new challenge, a few hardy walkers had already completed the full circuit within months of the Wales Coast Path's opening.

But whether you choose to walk the whole coast path in one go, in occasional sections, or a few miles at a time, you're in for a real treat. There's something new around every corner, and you'll discover places that can only

Gronant Dunes, Denbighshire

be reached on foot. Visually stunning and rich in both history and wildlife, the coast path promises ever-changing views, soaring cliffs and spacious beaches, sea caves and arches, wildflowers, seabirds, seals and dolphins, as well as castles, cromlechs, coves and coastal pubs. It's a genuinely special landscape.

This visual and ecological richness is recognised nationally and internationally. In fact, the Wales Coast Path runs through 1 Marine Nature Reserve, 1 Geopark, 2 National Parks, 3 Areas of Outstanding Natural Beauty, 3 World Heritage Sites, 7 official and unofficial nudist beaches, 11 National Nature Reserves, 14 Heritage Coasts, 17 Special Protection Areas, 21 Special Areas of Conservation, 23 Historic Landscapes, 42 Blue Flag beaches, and 111 marine Sites of Special Scientific Interest. Large stretches of coast are also managed and protected by Wildlife Trusts, the RSPB and the National Trust.

Long-distance walkers will enjoy the unbroken path, the solitude, the coast's constantly changing moods and the back-to-nature challenge. Holiday and weekend walkers can recharge their batteries, see something new, and regain an ever more necessary sense of perspective. Families can potter, play and explore. And locals can walk the dog, jog, get fit and rediscover their home patch. Whatever your preferences, the Wales Coast Path promises something for everyone.

All or Part?

So, what's the best way to walk the Wales Coast Path? The 870 mile/1400 kilometre route covers the whole of the Welsh seaboard and is the longest and probably the best of all Britain's long-distance challenges.

But of course, not everyone has the time, energy or inclination to walk it all at once. Instead, most people start with a short stretch, discover they love it, and come back for more.

Section by section

1 North Wales Coast

2 Isle of Anglesey

3 Llŷn Peninsula

4 Cardigan Bay & Ceredigion

5 Pembrokeshire

6 Carmarthen Bay & Gower

7 South Wales Coast

1. North Wales Coast

Chester to Bangor
80 miles/125 kilometres
7 Day Sections

Undulating coast, vast Dee Estuary, traditional seaside towns, limestone headland, and Conwy mountain

2. Isle of Anglesey

Circuit of island from Menai Bridge
125 miles/200 kilometres
12 Day Sections

Grand coastal scenery from tidal straits to bays, estuaries, dunes and cliffs. Area of Outstanding Natural Beauty

3. Llŷn Peninsula

Bangor to Porthmadog
110 miles/180 kilometres
9 Day Sections

Unspoilt peninsula with bays, coves and cliffs, tipped by Bardsey Island. Area of Outstanding Natural Beauty

4. Cardigan Bay & Ceredigion

Porthmadog to Cardigan
140 miles/225 kilometres
12 Day Sections

Low-lying dunes and big estuaries followed by steeper, grassy sea cliffs with dramatic coves and bays

5. Pembrokeshire

Cardigan to Amroth
186 miles/300 kilometres
14 Day Sections

Varied, beautiful, popular. The Pembrokeshire Coastal Path is a National Trail and coastal National Park

6. Carmarthen Bay & Gower

Tenby to Swansea
130 miles/210 kilometres
12 Day Sections

Long sandy beaches, tidal estuaries, dramatic rocky coast. Area of Outstanding Natural Beauty

7. South Wales Coast

Swansea to Chepstow
115 miles/185 kilometres
11 Day Sections

Traditional beach resorts, seafaring and industrial landscapes.
Heritage Coast, National Nature Reserves

Grand coast: *The mouth of the River Dee with Talacre, Barkby Beach and Gronant Dunes*

Wales: Top to Bottom

Walking the whole 870 miles/1400 kilometres of the Wales Coast Path in one go is an increasingly popular challenge. Some people have even run all the way. By a curious coincidence, the overall distance is almost exactly the same as Britain's famous top-to-bottom route, from John o' Groats to Land's End — a very long way.

The Wales Coast Path will take you from the outskirts of Chester, down the broad Dee estuary, along the North Wales coast with its traditional seaside resorts and impressive limestone headlands at Little and Great Orme, past Conwy Castle, over Conwy Mountain and on along the wooded Menai Strait. The path then loops around the rugged, offshore Isle of Anglesey, or Ynys Môn, passes the walled town of Caernarfon and its castle before heading around the remote Llŷn Peninsula with Bardsey Island balanced at its tip. From Criccieth and Porthmadog the path pushes south past Harlech Castle — kissing the western rim of the Snowdonia National Park — and on down the majestic sweep of Cardigan Bay with its beautiful, open estuaries. It then rounds Pembrokeshire — Britain's only coastal National Park — with

its sparkling bays and lofty cliffs. Striding through Carmarthenshire and crossing the wide Tywi and Tâf estuaries, the path curves around the lovely Gower Peninsula into Swansea Bay. Beyond the striking Glamorgan Heritage Coast, the path runs along the Cardiff Bay waterfront to Cardiff, the lively capital of Wales. From there, it's only a short stretch alongside the broad Severn Estuary to the pretty market town of Chepstow on the Welsh-English border and the southern end of the Wales Coast Path.

Only the fittest, most determined walkers can hope to complete the entire path in 6-7 weeks, averaging 20 or so miles a day.

At a more leisurely pace — allowing time to soak up the atmosphere and enjoy the views, and with regular pauses to watch the wildlife, swim, enjoy a quiet drink or visit some of the fascinating places along the way — you should allow around three months for the whole trip.

Remember, though, the Wales Coast Path is a challenging route with plenty of rough ground, narrow paths and ups-and-downs (an overall total ascent and descent of 95,800 feet/ 29,200 metres). There are tempting detours and places to see along the way, too. So it's perhaps best to plan slightly shorter and more realistic daily distances than you might ordinarily cover.

You should also allow extra time for the unexpected, to rest or to hole up in bad weather. As a rule of thumb, it's better to be ahead of schedule, with time to enjoy the experience, rather than always having to push ahead to reach the next overnight stop.

The Official Guidebooks in this series break the path down into seven main sections (see the map on page 10), each of which is then sub-divided into carefully-planned 'Day Sections' — usually averaging around 10-15 miles each. These typically start and finish either in, or near easy-to-reach towns, villages or settlements, many of them on bus routes, and with shops, pubs, restaurants, cafés and places to stay nearby.

No matter how long it takes, walking the whole of the Wales Coast Path is a real achievement. For most of us, it would be the walk of a lifetime.

Walking around Wales a bit at a time

Yet, understandably, most people don't want to walk the whole Path in one go. Instead, they prefer to do it bit by bit, often over several years: during annual and bank holidays, over long weekends, or as the whim takes them. Done in this leisurely fashion, the walk becomes a project to ponder, plan, and take pleasure in.

A popular way to enjoy the path is to book a short holiday close to a section of the path, and do a series of day walks along the surrounding coast, returning to your base each night.

Penmon Lighthouse and Puffin Island, off the south-east coast of Anglesey.

Rock with a view: *Enjoying the view to the Great Orme from the Little Orme*

Some people like to catch a train (especially along the North Wales Coast), bus or taxi to the start of their day's walk and then walk back (see the information at the start of each Day Section).

Another approach is to drive to the end of your planned section and then get a pre-booked local taxi to take you back to the start; this costs only a few pounds and lets you to walk in one direction at your own pace.

If you're planning to walk a section over several days before returning to your starting point by bus or train, call Traveline on **0870 6082608** or visit **www.traveline-cymru.org.uk** for help with timetables and itineraries.

Best time to go?

Britain's main walking season runs from Easter to the end of September. Although the Wales Coast Path is delightful throughout the year, the best walking weather tends to be in late spring as well as early and late summer.

Although the Easter holiday is busy, spring is otherwise a quiet time of year. The days are lengthening and the weather getting steadily warmer. Migrant birds and basking sharks are returning to Wales from farther south. The weather is also likely to be dry.

Early summer is ideal for walking. May and June enjoy the greatest

Rugged coast: The tiny hamlet of Porthdinllaen on the Llŷn Peninsula

number of sunshine hours per day (the average for May is 225 hours, and for June 210 hours) and the lowest rainfall of the year (average for May is 50mm, June is 51mm). You'll also have the accompaniment of a spectacular array of spring flowers and the chance to see breeding sea birds at their best.

High summer is the busiest season, particularly during the school holidays in July and August. Both the beaches and the Coast Path are likely to be packed in places. Finding somewhere to stay at short notice can be tricky, too — so it's best to book well in advance. However, the long sunny days are certainly attractive, and you can often walk in shorts and a T-shirt.

By September most visitors have returned home, and you'll have the path largely to yourself. The weather remains good and the sea is still warm enough for swimming. Sunny days often stretch into September, with the first of the winter storms arriving in late September and October. Autumn also means the coastal trees and bracken are slowly turning from green to red, orange and gold.

Winter brings shorter, colder days with less sunlight and other disadvantages: unpredictable weather, stormy seas, high winds and even gales,

along with closed cafés and accommodation. But for experienced walkers, the cooler days can bring peace and solitude and a heightened sense of adventure.

Welsh weather

Like the rest of Britain, Wales is warmed by the Gulf Stream's ocean current and enjoys a temperate climate. This is particularly true of the Llŷn Peninsula. Because Wales lies in the west of Britain, the weather is generally mild but damp. Low pressure fronts typically come in off the Irish Sea from the west and southwest, hitting the coast first and then moving inland to the east. This means rain and wet weather can occur at any time of year, so you should always take good waterproofs and spare clothes with you.

For more weather or a five-day forecast, visit **www.metoffice.com** or **www.bbc.co.uk/weather**. Several premium-rate national 'Weatherlines' give up-to-date forecasts, and the Snowdonia and Pembrokeshire National Parks websites provide local information, too.

Which direction?

The Official Guide books give directions from north to south, starting in Chester and ending in Chepstow. This means walkers will enjoy the sun on their faces for much of the way. Most luggage transfer services also run in this direction. Nonetheless, the path can be tackled in either direction. It's just easier to go with the flow.

Which section?

Choosing which part of the Wales Coast Path to walk depends in part on where you live, how long you've got, and the kind of scenery you prefer.

Sections vary considerably. Arry Beresford-Webb, the first person to run the entire Path in 2012 said, "I was stunned by the diversity of the path. Each section felt like I was going through a different country."

Some stretches are fairly wild, while others are more developed. Parts of the Isle of Anglesey, Llŷn Peninsula, Cardigan Bay and Pembrokeshire are often remote and away from large settlements. Other stretches, such as North Wales or the South Wales Coast around Swansea, Cardiff and Newport are busier, and often close to popular seaside towns or industry.

The terrain varies too. Much of the North Wales Coast is low-lying but punctuated with occasional headlands; as are much of Cardigan Bay, Carmarthen Bay, and parts of the Glamorgan Heritage Coast.

In contrast, the Isle of Anglesey, Llŷn Peninsula, Pembrokeshire and Gower are often rocky with high sea cliffs, dramatic headlands, offshore islands and intimate coves.

Self sufficient or supported?

The other key decision for walkers is whether to arrange everything yourself or let someone else do it for you. For many people, devising their own itinerary and working out how to travel and where to stay is part of the fun. Others prefer to let one of the specialist walking holiday companies create the itinerary, book accommodation, arrange luggage transfers, meals, and side trips. The main companies are listed at the back of the book.

Accommodation

There are plenty of places to stay within easy reach of the Wales Coast Path all around Wales. Most walkers either camp or stay in bed and breakfast accommodation; usually a mix of the two. There are plenty of hostels and bunkhouses along the way but, unfortunately, they are too unevenly spaced to provide accommodation every night.

Accommodation may be fully booked during peak holiday seasons, so it's advisable to book well ahead. Local Tourist Information Centres (TICs) will often know all the local accommodation providers, know who has vacancies, and can help with booking. For late, or emergency on the spot bookings, it's also worth contacting the TICs listed at the start of each Day Section.

Backpacking

Backpacking adds an extra dimension to the walking experience: being outdoors for days at a time, watching the sunrise and sunset, gazing at the stars overhead without artificial light getting in the way. But don't underestimate how much a heavy pack can slow you down. The secret is to travel as light as possible; the lightest tent or bivvy bag, a lightweight sleeping bag and waterproofs, and a single change of clothes.

There are plenty of official campsites along the busier sections of the Wales Coast Path. However, many are on small farms and may not advertise. Elsewhere campsites are often few and far between, and may need searching for. During peak season some may also be full, so it's advisable to book ahead. But remember, most sites are closed during the winter (typically from November to Easter, and often longer).

Unofficial 'wild camping' is a grey area. There is no legal right in Britain to 'wild camp' anywhere, including alongside the path. Every scrap of land in Britain belongs to someone, and many landowners frown on campers. So it makes sense to ask before pitching.

Shell Island, or Mochras, near Harlech, in Gwynedd, North Wales

Sand and sea: Looking towards Barmouth across the Mawddach Estuary

Unofficially, however, overnight camping is usually tolerated, so long as you pitch a small tent unobtrusively in the evening, and pack up and leave early the next morning, without leaving a trace.

Alternatively, there are popular luggage transfer services on the more established stretches of the path. For a small fee, they will pick up your rucksack and other bags and transport them to the end of your day's walk. A list of luggage transfer companies appears at the back of the book.

Clothes, boots and backpack

For those new to long distance walking, it's worth emphasising the benefits of comfortable walking boots and suitable clothing. Walking continuously, day after day, puts extra pressures on your feet. Be prepared for changes in the weather, too. Carry waterproofs and remember that several thin layers allow you to adjust your clothing as conditions change.

Checking the weather forecast before you set off each day will help you decide what to wear. If you're in the car, it's worth taking a selection of clothing for different conditions, and deciding what to wear and carry immediately before you start.

Onshore breezes can mask the strength of the sun. To avoid sunburn, or even sunstroke, remember to slap on some sunscreen and wear a hat.

Other things to take, depending on weight, include: maps, water bottle, lightweight walking poles, basic First Aid including plasters and antiseptic cream, penknife, head torch and spare batteries, chocolate, sweets or energy bars, toilet paper, a small camera, binoculars, mobile phone, and a pen and notebook. Don't forget some spare cash too; most places accept cards but finding a Cashpoint or somewhere that offers 'Cash Back' near the path can be tricky.

Food and Drink

Although the Official Guides try to start and end each Day Section at places with amenities, some stretches are nonetheless remote and may have few places to buy food or drink. This may be the case for several days in a row. So it makes sense to plan ahead and carry enough supplies with you.

Conversely, other stretches are well supplied with shops, pubs, cafés, restaurants and takeaways; these are indicated at the start of each Day Section.

Maps

The maps in this book are reproduced to scale from the magenta-covered

Ordnance Survey Landranger 1:50,000 series, enhanced with additional information. The official route of the Wales Coast Path is highlighted in orange. The numbers on the maps correspond to those in the route description for each Day Section.

It's also worth taking the larger scale, orange-covered Ordnance Survey Explorer 1:25,000 maps with you. These show additional features such as Access Land, field boundaries, springs and wells.

Both scales of OS maps now have the official route of the Wales Coast Path marked on them as a line composed of a series of diamond symbols. Grid squares on both series of maps represent one square kilometre.

The relevant maps for each Day Section are listed at the beginning of each chapter. The grid references given in this book for the start and finish of each Day Section are from the Ordnance Survey maps.

The mouth of the Dyfi estuary

Beautiful bay: *Walking on the Wales Coast Path near Worm's Head, on the Gower Peninsula*

Route finding

For the most part, the Wales Coast Path follows a single official route. In a few places, there are both official and unofficial alternative routes. Otherwise, the path hugs the coast as far is practically and legally possible, occasionally diverting inland around private estates, nature reserves, natural obstacles, estuaries, gunnery ranges and so on. The definitive route, and any occasional changes are notified on the official Wales Coast Path website.

The path uses a mixture of public rights of way: footpaths, bridleways and byways as well as lanes, open access land, beaches and some permissive paths. On most sections, the route is well-used and clear. In remote or under-used areas, however, walkers will need to pay closer attention to the maps and directions in this book.

Fingerposts and waymarkers

The Wales Coast Path is clearly signed and waymarked with its own distinctive logo: a white dragon-tailed seashell on a blue background surrounded by a yellow circlet bearing the words 'Llwybr Arfordir Cymru - Wales Coast Path'. Look for the wood or metal fingerposts at main access points, in towns, on roadsides and lanes, and at key junctions.

Clear waymarking: *The route is clearly waymarked with plastic roundels fixed to stiles, gateposts, fences and walls*

Elsewhere, the route is clearly waymarked with plastic roundels fixed to stiles, gateposts, fences and walls. In many places the Wales Coast Path waymarkers sit alongside others for already established routes — such as the Isle of Anglesey Coastal Path or the Pembrokeshire Coast Path National Trail. In

Official route waymarkers

Official alternative route waymarker

some areas these local waymarkers are still more in evidence than the official Wales Coast Path ones; and on some stretches, waymarking remains patchy.

Alternative routes

Two sorts of alternative route are described in the guides. The first are the **official alternative routes** that avoid remote or challenging sections; and more attractive routes that, for example, provide better views or get farther away from motor traffic.

The second are our own **unofficial alternative routes**. Many of these are beach routes below the high water mark that by their nature are not permanently available, and so do not qualify as part of the 'official route'. Others are alternative high level routes or simply 'better' or more attractive, in our opinion. Both the **official** and **unofficial alternative routes** are shown on the maps in this book as a broken orange highlight.

Detours

The directions also describe **detours** to places of interest that we think you won't want to miss. These are usually short, off the main Path, there-and-back routes, typically of no more than a kilometre or so in each direction. Suggested detours can take you to anything from a special pub, castle or church to a stunning view or waterfall. If you've got the time, they bring an extra dimension to the walk. Detours are shown on the maps as a blue broken highlight.

Temporary diversions

There may be occasional or seasonal temporary inland diversions. The reasons for them vary from land management and public safety: forestry work, cliff falls, landslips and floods, to wildlife conservation: protecting seal breeding sites, bird roosts and nesting sites, and so on. Details of the latest permanent and temporary diversions can be found on the official Wales Coast Path website under 'Route Changes'.

Tides and tide tables

As much as five percent of the Wales Coast Path runs along the foreshore, between mean high and low water. These sections are naturally affected by the tide. On the whole, the official Wales Coast Path avoids beaches and estuaries. However, beaches often provide time-honoured, direct and pleasant walking routes and are usually safely accessible, except for around 1½ hours either side of high tide. If the tide is in, or you're in any doubt, take the inland route instead.

Occasional streams and tidal creeks may also be crossed at low tide but be impassable at high water. So it is a good idea to carry tide tables with you and consult them before you set out each day. They are widely available for around £1 from coastal TICs, shops and newsagents.

Several websites also give accurate tidal predictions for locations around the UK, including downloadable five day predictions. Useful websites include: **www.bbc.co.uk/weather/coast_and_sea/tide_tables** and **www.easytide.ukho.gov.uk**.

Coastal town: *Tenby and St Catherine's Island in south Pembrokeshire*

Safety advice

If you're new to long-distance walking, or in one of the remoter areas, please remember:

- Wear walking boots and warm, waterproof clothing.
- Take food and drink.
- Mobile signals are patchy along much of the path; let someone know where you are heading and when you expect to arrive.
- If you decide to walk along a beach, always check tide tables.
- Stay on the path and away from cliff edges.
- Take extra care in windy and/or wet conditions.
- Always supervise children and dogs.
- Follow local signs and diversions.

Emergencies

In an emergency, call 999 or 112 and ask for the service your require: Ambulance, Police, Fire or Coastguard.

Tell them your location as accurately as possible (give an OS grid reference, if possible; and look for named landmarks), how many people are in your party, and the nature of the problem.

Remember, though, that mobile signals may be poor or absent in some areas. Some coastal car parks and main beach access points have emergency telephones. Coastal pubs and shops may also have phones you can ask to use in an emergency.

Who manages the coast path?

The Wales Coast Path is co-ordinated at a national level by Natural Resources Wales and managed on the ground by the sixteen local authorities and two National Parks through which it passes.

Funding has come from the Welsh Government, the European Regional Development Fund and the local authorities themselves.

For more details, see: **http://naturalresourceswales.gov.uk**

The **Best** of the **North Wales Coast**

It is easy to understand why the **North Wales Coast** has attracted visitors for centuries. It is vibrant and varied, with plenty to offer walkers, from wide estuaries, sand dunes and long sandy beaches to spectacular limestone headlands and heather-clad moorland with magnificent sea views. Along the way you'll pass medieval castles, Victorian seaside resorts with elegant piers and promenades, picturesque quaysides and working harbours. Traditional fishing boats bob in the water alongside modern pleasure craft, and the estuaries are a veritable paradise for birdwatchers.

Flint Castle

Bettisfield

Dee Estuary

Talacre lighthouse

Gronant dunes

Rhyl beach

Great Orme

Conwy Castle

Conwy Mountain

Bangor Pier

The North Wales Coast
Part of the **Wales Coast Path**

Walking the North Wales Coast will surprise and delight. The coast has been justifiably popular with holidaymakers old and young since Victorian times but has also a rich maritime heritage. It was an important shipping route linking the north west with Ireland and beyond. Harbours, shipyards and industries developed along the coast and the fishing industry also flourished.

It is one of the most accessible stretches of the Wales Coast Path, and includes long stretches of flat promenade with plenty of seats, suitable for the less active visitor, including wheelchair users and young families with buggies. There is also excellent public transport along the whole route, with train stations at regular intervals and frequent bus services.

The Wales Coast Path begins at the Welsh border on the River Dee a couple of miles outside the historic City of Chester, then follows the river into the widening estuary, passing expanses of mudflats that are feeding grounds for thousands of wildfowl and waders.

From the mouth of the estuary by Talacre lighthouse, the path leads along the beach and through the dunes at Gronant, then along promenades through a string of Victorian seaside resorts. The route then climbs the Little Orme, before following the sweeping promenade of elegant Llandudno to the magnificent Great Orme. Here the path follows Marine Drive, built as a Victorian carriage route, then continues along the coast to the Medieval walled town of Conwy.

At Conwy there is a choice of routes to Llanfairechan: the more challenging upland route over the heather-clad moorland of Conwy Mountain, or a more gentle walk hugging the coast around Morfa Conwy and Penmaenmawr, with the mountains as a backdrop. From Llanfairfechan, the peaceful path stays close to the water's edge with superb views across the Menai Strait, eventually following a disused railway line into Bangor.

Gorse and heather on Conwy Mountain

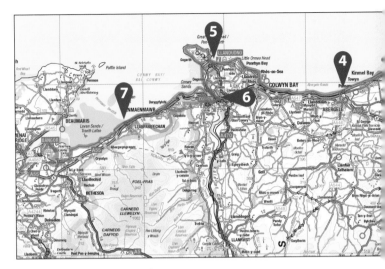

Walking the North Wales coast

The North Wales Coast section of the Wales Coast Path runs for 76 miles/ 180 kilometres between the Welsh border* near Chester to Bangor, on the Menai Straits. In turn, it is split into seven logical day sections, most around 10-15 miles/17-24 kilometres. Each starts and finishes at or close to somewhere attractive and accessible, with good or reasonable facilities. The numbered day sections are shown on the map below.

*Our directions begin in Chester as that is the natural place to start in terms of access and facilities.

Near Morfa Aber

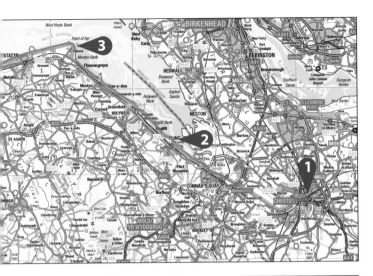

Day Section	Distance	Start	Finish
Day Section 1 Chester to Flint	13 miles 21km	Chester Station SJ 413 670	Flint Castle SJ 247 733
Day Section 2 2a Flint to Talacre low route 2b with optional woodland section	13½ miles 22km 14½ miles 24km	Flint Castle SJ 247 733	Talacre, Sta Rd SJ 125 848
Day Section 3 Talacre to Pensarn	13 miles 21km	Talacre SJ 125 848	Pensarn station SH 946 787
Day Section 4 Pensarn to Llandudno	12½ miles 20km	Pensarn station SH 946 787	Llandudno Pier SH 783 829
Day Section 5 Llandudno to Conwy	8½ miles 14km	Llandudno Pier SH 783 829	Conwy SH 783 776
Day Section 6a Conwy to Llanfairfechan low	9 miles 14.5km	Conwy SH 783 776	Llanfairfechan SH 679 754
Day Section 6b Conwy to Llanfairfechan high	11 miles 18km	Conwy SH 783 776	Llanfairfechan SH 679 754
Day Section 7 Llanfairfechan to Bangor	9½ miles 15.5km	Llanfairfechan SH 679 754	Bangor Pier SH 585 732

Distance chart for key locations along the path

Miles (upper right) / **Kilometres** (lower left)

	Bangor	Abergwyngregyn	Llanfairfechan	Penmaenmawr	Conwy	Deganwy	Llandudno West Shore	Llandudno North Shore	Rhos-on-Sea	Colwyn Bay	Pensarn	Rhyl	Prestatyn	Talacre	Ffynnongroyw	Mostyn	Greenfield	Bagillt	Flint	Shotton	Chester (border)
Chester (border)	76	69	66	63	58	56	54	50	45	43	37	33	29	24	22	20	17	14	11	5	
Shotton	71	64	61	58	52	51	49	44	39	38	32	27	23	19	16	14	11	8	6		9
Flint	65	58	55	52	47	45	43	39	34	32	26	22	18	13	11	9	6	3		9	18
Bagillt	62	55	52	50	44	42	40	36	31	29	23	19	15	11	8	6	3		5	14	22
Greenfield	60	53	50	47	41	40	38	33	28	27	21	16	12	8	5	3		4	9	18	27
Mostyn	56	49	46	44	38	36	34	30	25	23	17	13	9	5	2		5	10	14	23	32
Ffynnongroyw	55	48	45	42	36	35	33	28	23	22	16	11	7	3		3	8	13	18	26	35
Talacre	52	45	42	39	33	32	30	25	20	19	13	8	4		4	7	13	17	22	31	39
Prestatyn	47	40	37	35	29	27	25	21	16	15	8	4		7	12	14	20	24	29	38	47
Rhyl	44	37	34	31	25	24	22	17	12	11	5		6	13	17	20	26	30	35	44	52
Pensarn	39	32	29	26	21	19	17	12	7	6		8	14	21	25	28	33	38	42	51	60
Colwyn Bay	33	26	23	20	18	13	11	6	1		10	18	23	31	35	38	43	47	52	61	70
Rhos-on-Sea	32	25	22	19	13	12	10	5		2	12	19	25	32	37	40	45	49	54	63	72
Llandudno N Shore	27	20	17	14	8	7	5		8	10	20	27	33	40	45	48	53	57	62	71	80
Llandudno N Shore	22	15	12	9	4	2		8	16	18	27	35	41	48	53	55	61	65	70	79	87
Deganwy	20	13	10	7	2		3	11	19	21	30	38	44	51	56	58	64	68	73	82	91
Conwy	18	11	8	6		3	6	14	21	23	33	41	47	54	58	61	67	71	76	84	93
Penmaenmawr	13	6	3		9	12	15	22	30	32	42	50	56	63	67	70	75	80	85	93	102
Llanfairfechan	10	3		5	13	16	19	27	35	37	47	54	60	67	72	75	80	84	89	98	107
Abergwyngregyn	7		5	10	18	21	24	33	42	43	53	59	65	73	77	80	85	89	94	103	112
Bangor		11	16	21	29	32	35	43	51	58	63	70	76	83	88	91	96	100	105	114	123

Distances are approximate to the nearest mile/kilometre

Day Sections

1: Chester to Flint

Distance: 13 miles/21 kilometres

Terrain: Flat and easy walking alongside the River Dee, mainly following cycleway, with roadside walking between Connah's Quay and Oakenholt, then natural path across saltmarsh

Points of interest: Queensferry and Flint Bridges, remains of wooden wharves, Connah's Quay Docks, birdlife on Dee Estuary and saltmarsh, Flint Castle, sculptures and interpretation along the route

Note: Plenty of accommodation and all facilities in Chester, B&B at Oakenholt, toilets, post office, banks, pubs, cafés, takeaways, shops in Flint. Good public transport by train or bus

2a: Flint to Talacre (low route via Mostyn)

Distance: 13½ miles/22 kilometres

Terrain: Easy, level paths above shoreline and along stone embankment with some roadside walking between Mostyn and Ffynongroyw.

Points of interest: Wide views across estuary, Bettisfield and Greenfield docks, (detour up Greenfield Valley to St Winefride's Well in Holywell), Abakhan Mill, grounded Duke of Lancaster ferry, coal mining heritage, Point of Ayr bird reserve, sculptures and interpretation along the route

Note: Pub at Llannerch-y-mor and cafe at Abakhan Mill, hotel, pubs and shop in Ffynnongroyw, cafés, shop and pubs at Talacre

2b: Flint to Talacre (optional high route through woodland)

Distance: 14½ miles/24 kilometres

Terrain: Short diversion to avoid walking along main road at Mostyn, leads through a delightful wooded valley

Points of interest: Waterfalls and old mill

3: Talacre to Pensarn, Abergele

Distance: 13 miles/21 kilometres

Terrain: Easy, natural paths along the beach and through the dunes to Prestatyn, then promenade to Pensarn

Points of interest: Talacre Lighthouse, beach and dunes, wide views, sand dune flora and fauna, little tern colony at Gronant, windfarms, beaches and seaside resorts

Note: Plenty of accommodation, bank, post office, pubs, cafés, takeaways and shops in Prestatyn, Rhyl and Abergele

4: Pensarn to Llandudno

Distance: 12½ miles/ 20 kilometres

Terrain: Easy walking on tarmac pavement and promenade all the way to Rhos on Sea, then natural path with some ascent over the Little Orme down to Llandudno promenade

Points of interest: Beaches and seaside resorts, windfarms, Porth Eirias, St Teilo's Chapel, Little Orme, grey seals, Llandudno seafront

Morfa Conwy beach

Wide sandy beaches: *Talacre is a popular beach venue in the summer*

Note: Promenade café at Pensarn, accommodation, pubs, cafés, fish and chips, post office and shops in Abergele, Colywn Bay, Rhos on Sea and Llandudno

5: Llandudno to Conwy

Distance: 8½miles/ 14 kilometres

Terrain: Tarmac path throughout, following pavement round Marine Drive alongside West Shore and Deganwy (alternative option on grassy paths over the Great Orme with steep ascent and descent)

Points of interest: Llandudno Pier, tramway, cable car, Great Orme Copper Mines, Great Orme - views, cliffs, wild goats, seabirds and limestone flora, marina, Conwy Castle and walled town, Conwy harbour, mussel industry, Smallest House in Great Britain

Note: Accommodation and all amenities in Llanduno, café on Marine Drive, accommodation, shops and refreshments in Deganwy and Conwy

6a: Conwy to Llanfairfechan – coastal route

Distance: 9 miles/ 14.5 kilometres

Terrain: Easy, flat path alongside estuary to Conwy Marina, sandy and pebbly paths around Morfa Conwy, tarmac path to Llanfairfechan

Sweeping bays: *View along Llandudno beach to the Great Orme*

Points of interest: Bodlondeb Woods, Conwy Marina, Morfa Conwy sand dunes, views of the estuary and Conwy Mountain, Penmaenmawr beaches and heritage of granite quarrying.

Note: A range of accommodation, post office, pubs, cafés, takeaways, shops in Penmaenmawr and Llanfairfechan.

6b: Conwy to Llanfairfechan – upland route

Distance: 11 miles/ 18 kilometres

Terrain: Challenging, upland walking on natural paths with lots of ascent and descent, some steep sections.

Points of interest: Superb views to coast and Snowdonia, moorland flora and fauna, Carneddau ponies, Castell Caer Seion hillfort, Prehistoric standing stones and burial mounds, quarry remains, Victorian Jubilee Path

Note: B&Bs, post office, pubs, cafés, takeaways, shops in Penmaenmawr; pubs, restaurant and hotels in Dwygyfylchi; B&Bs, campsite and bunkhouse, shops, pubs, post office, takeaways in Llanfairfechan, plus Beach Pavilion and Beach Hut cafes on promenade at Llanfairfechan.

7: Llanfairfechan to Bangor

Distance: 9½ miles/ 15.5 kilometres

Terrain: Easy, flat walking on surfaced path, then natural paths alongside nature reserves, (occasional stoney sections), tarmac pavements and road-side walking (care needed), then pleasant path through woodland along a disused railway line path into Bangor

Points of interest: Wetland nature reserves, birdlife on Traeth Lavan, views across Menai Strait to Anglesey, Penrhyn Castle, Bangor Pier, Bangor Cathedral and town

Note: Plenty of accommodation, bank, post office, pubs, cafés, shops in Bangor.

View from Conwy Castle

Limited for time? The **North Wales Coast** in a nutshell

If you have limited time to explore this section of the Wales Coast Path —
perhaps a weekend, or even just a day, then these key parts of the path are
unmissable.

For a delightful one day walk, try the section between Flint Castle and
Talacre along the widening Dee Estuary. Walk beside the estuary round
Flint Point and along Bagillt Cop to Greenfield, enjoying the wide views,
then continue towards Mostyn Docks. Detour inland to enjoy the tumbling
woodland waterfalls and then continue to the beach at Talacre.

For a superb two-day walk, the section between Conwy and Bangor is
recommended, taking the upland route on the first day over Conwy Mountain. This exhilarating mountain walk is more challenging than the coastal
routes but offers stunning views. Day 2 is more gentle but equally enjoyable,
hugging the coast to Bangor.

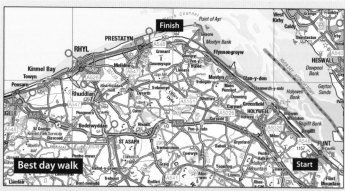

Best day walk
Along the Dee Estuary

Flint Castle to Talacre 14.5 miles/ 24 kilometres

Join the Coast Path by the castle and walk alongside the estuary. Detour inland at the Llety Hotel through woodland and pasture. Rejoin the coastal route at Ffynnongroyw and follow to Talacre (Day section 2b). Parking at Flint Castle; regular bus services between Flint, Ffynnongroyw and Talacre.

Bagillt Cop

Best weekend walk
Over Conwy Mountain to Llanfairfechan then hug the coast to Bangor

Conwy to Bangor: 20.5 miles/ 34 kilometres

Day One: From Conwy harbour, follow the upland route over Conwy Mountain to Llanfairfechan (Day section 6b) **Day Two:** From Llanfairfechan follow the coastline, walking on natural paths between wetland nature reserves and Traeth Lavan with wonderful views across the Menai Strait (Day Section 7). You can use the train from Bangor or Llanfairfechan to return to Conwy.

Conwy Mountain

A brief history of the
North Wales Coast

From standing stones and Medieval castles to ports, harbours and seaside holidays

People have been drawn to the North Wales Coast for many thousands of years. The high mountains, dense forest and swamp of inland Wales were impenetrable so prehistoric settlers came by sea. The coastal waters continued to be an important trading route as well as providing a bountiful larder of fish and shellfish. Ports developed and communities grew up around them. Entrepreneurs opened mines, quarries and factories, making the most of the natural resources and navigable seas. The medieval castles positioned strategically along the coast bear testament to its military importance too. Later visitors had more peaceful motives. Day trippers first started to come by paddle steamer in the 1820s and the sandy beaches with their mountain backdrop have been attracting visitors ever since.

Standing stones and stone axes

The coastal area was widely used by prehistoric peoples, firstly hunter gatherers, living in caves such as those on the Great Orme, and later Stone Age settlers who who began to clear land and farm. Their stone axe factories on the hillside above Penmaemawr and Llanfairfechan were some of the largest in Britain.

When bronze – a mix of copper and tin - was introduced to Britain about 4000 years ago, the copper found on the Great Orme was really important and the size of the mine workings were unparalled anywhere in Western Europe. The numerous standing stones, stone circles and cairns on the mountains and hills overlooking the coast are reminders of the importance of the North Wales Coast for these earlier peoples.

The Romans were also drawn by the mineral wealth of the area. Chester was an important Roman city and from here, the 20th Legion marched out along the coast, establishing outposts at Prestatyn where the remains of a Roman Bath-house have been excavated and at Oakenholt, near Flint, where they smelted lead that had been mined on Halkyn Mountain.

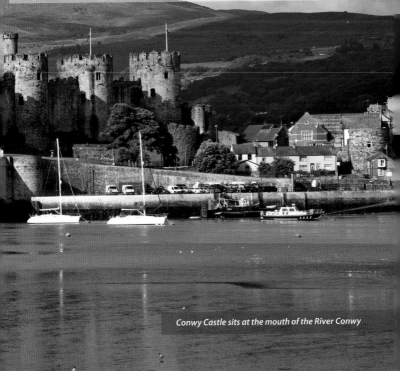

Conwy Castle sits at the mouth of the River Conwy

Prehistoric landscape: *Standing stones above Penmaenmawr*

Saints and pilgrims

Across Wales the sixth century was known as the Age of Saints, with Christian missionaries and itinerant monks, arriving to convert the pagan tribes. Many Celtic Saints are associated with this coastline, including St Trillo who landed at Rhos on Sea, St Tudno who settled on the Great Orme, and St Beuno and his niece, Saint Winefride, who are associated with Holywell. Pilgrims flocked to seek cures or do penance at St Winefride's Well. Many came by sea from Liverpool and Lancashire, landing at Greenfield Dock.

Military might

The sea was important for military purposes too - giving an easy route into and out of North Wales for invaders and raiders. For centuries the coast was the site of battles and military action. There have been numerous fortifications along the coast. Some were originally Welsh strongholds, such as Deganwy Castle, reputedly a Dark Age base for the King of Gwynedd, and medieval Ewloe Castle near the Welsh border, built by Llywelyn the Last to control the routes to Chester. Others were English; the castles at Flint, Rhuddlan and Conwy were built by Edward I as the first of his 'iron ring' of castles during his conquest of North Wales.

In the 17th century, the Conwy and Flint castles were garrisoned once again in the Civil Wars and became Royalist strongholds. Both were beseiged by the Parliamentarian forces and held out for several months before surrendering. After the hostilities had ended the castles were slighted to ensure they could not be used for miliatry purposes again.

The coast had a role during the Second World War too. The coastal waters were used to test submarines built at Cammell Laird's in Birkenhead, including the doomed Thetis which tragically sank during its maiden voyage. Pillboxes, small, squat concrete forts, were built along the coast to defend the approach to Liverpool from North Wales in case of an anticipated German invasion. Several still remain near Queensferry, at Talacre and Llandudno.

The Mulberry Harbours, the floating landing stages developed for the D Day landings, were developed and constructed at Morfa Conwy. RAF pilots practised their bombing at Talacre beach and large numbers of evacuees from Merseyside lived in the holiday homes in the dunes. Many others were evacuated to towns and villages along the coast.

Aerial view of Flint Castle

Cockles and mussels

The rich waters of the estuaries provided a important source of food for the coastal communities from prehistoric times. Over time, fishing became more organised with small fleets working from the harbours and havens along the coast.

Prawns were a speciality catch in Conwy Bay. Some fishermen used 'nobby prawners', many of which were built at Crossfield's boatyard in Conwy. In the early 20th century, forty of these little wooden saling boats fished Conwy Bay and a fleet of 12 trawlers worked from Conwy until the 1960s.

The Dee was renowned for its salmon, and fishermen from Flint and Connah's Quay were eager to get the prized but expensive salmon licences. Summer was the salmon fishing season, with flounders and shrimps mainly caught in the autumn. Salmon licences are no longer issued but some commercial fishing and shell-fish harvesting continues today. Dee Estuary cockles and Conwy mussels are highly prized. The volume and variety of fish caught is steadily increasing, as the water quality has improved since the closure of some of the polluting industries on the Dee. Sea angling is a popular sport for amateur fishermen along the coast.

Cockler moored in Flint Dock

Majestic ship: *The Kathleen and May was built at Connah's Quay*

Navigation and trade

The North Wales coast has been an important trade route for thousands of years, since prehistoric peoples traded stone axes, copper and bronze. Edward I built quays at Flint and Conwy to service his new castles. Chester, linked to the sea by the Dee Estuary, was the main medieval port for north west England. Over time the River Dee silted and Chester lost its importance but the building of the New Cut in 1737 brought the shipping to the Flintshire side of the estuary and a number of small ports and shipyards developed, including Connah's Quay.

Following the Industrial Revolution collieries were built at Bagillt, Mostyn and Point of Ayr to mine the rich coal seams that ran underneath the Dee Estuary. The last colliery closed in 1996 but energy generation continues to be an important part of the local industry today with a gas terminal and many wind turbines out at sea.

The coastal waters became a key shipping route to and from Ireland. Flintshire coal, limestone from Halkyn and Llanddulas, granite setts from Penmaenmawr and Welsh slate were important exports. Entreprenuers saw the opportunities that the navigable seas gave, building factories and processing plants along the Dee Estuary — ironworks, chemical plants and

Victorian elegance: *Llandudno Pier*

lead smelters. Tramways and railway branch lines were built to link inland industries with the coastal ports. Communities developed to house workers in the quarries, factories and ports.

The numbers and size of ships using these waters increased in the 18th and 19th centuries as Liverpool developed as a port, with many ships coming from America and across the world. These seas are treacherous and many lives have been lost. Lighthouses and beacons were erected to avert disaster, including the iconic Talacre lighthouse.

Shipping is greatly reduced nowadays but Mostyn Port still thrives. Airbus wings are transported by barge along the River Dee to Mostyn where they are transferred to a larger ship for the journey to France. Limestone is still transported by sea from Llanddulas and service boats for the offshore gas terminals and windfarms are commonly seen, along with the larger ferries and other ships from Liverpool, further out at sea. Further west, pleasure craft mix with the working boats, with marinas at Rhyl, Deganwy and Conwy for them to moor. Smaller sailing dinghies and canoes are also seen on the water around Penmaenmawr and the Menai Strait.

Seaside holidays

From the Victorian era the coast became a tourist destination. Paddle steamers brought the first tourists to the North Wales coast, drawn by the healthy sea air and the fashion for sea-bathing. Piers were built at at Llandudno, Rhyl, Rhos, Bangor, Menai Bridge, Beaumaris and thousands of Merseyside and Lancashire visitors were coming on day trips by steamer.

The opening of the Chester to Holyhead railway in 1848 brought increased visitors. Resorts like Prestatyn developed rapidly, with large numbers of hotels and boarding houses opening. By the Edwardian era, this coast was accessible for all. Paid holidays, half day Saturdays and a general increased standard of living had given more leisure time and the disposable income of the working classes had risen. Over 300,000 came by train each summer season!

Holiday tastes have changed, aided by car ownership and cheap flights, but the beaches are still busy in the summer months and the coast is popular for walking, kite surfing and cycling throughout the year.

Wildlife on the North Wales Coast

Among the many pleasures of walking the Wales Coast Path are the regular encounters with wildlife. Day by day, you'll come across a wealth of animals and plants, both common and uncommon. Much of the North Wales Coast is designated as a Special Area of Conservation to protect the wetland habitats that support such a wonderful range of wildlife. Keep your eyes peeled, and you've a good chance of seeing everything from wild goats, seabirds, orchids and choughs, to wading birds, Carneddau ponies and grey seals.

Horned poppy

Feral goat

Shelducks

Sea holly

Oystercatcher

Silver-studded blues

Sea bindweed

Little tern

Redshank

Pyramidal orchid

Waders, terns and wild goats

A wealth of wildlife thrives in the varied habitats of the North Wales Coast

The North Wales coast is outstanding for wildlife and is a great place for birdwatching throughout the year. The estuaries of the Rivers Dee, Conwy, Aber and Ogwen are internationally important for their birdlife but there are also miles of sand dunes and shingle, limestone grassland and cliffs on the Great and Little Orme together with wonderful heather moorland on the mountains above the coast, each with their own unique plants and animals.

The Dee Estuary is a fabulous place for wildlife, providing a refuge for over 100,000 wintering wildfowl and waders each year. In spring and summer too, it is an area where nature thrives alongside man

Iolo Williams

Mudflats and saltmarsh

Thousands of birds flock to the wide expanses of mudflats and saltmarsh. The estuaries may look like a barren wilderness but the oozing mud is fertile and full of life. Cockles, mussels, lugworms, small fish and a myriad of invertebrates provide a rich larder for the birds, seals, porpoises and dolphins.

Many birds remain all year and breed. Oystercatchers, curlew, and redshank are very common, in addition to large numbers of gulls. Large numbers of shelduck also breed on the estuaries and are often seen in pairs, feeding on the mudflats. Cormorants and shag are common too, often seen standing with outstretched wings or floating on the water between dives for fish.

In winter, the resident birds are joined by thousands of wading birds and wildfowl that migrate from the Arctic. Flocks of small waders, like dunlin and knot, scurry across the exposed mud, or, wheel into the sky when disturbed, their shrill calls breaking the silence. Thousands of ducks, including pintail, widgeon and smaller teal, also spend winter on these estuaries. Many can be seen on the sand banks at low tide.

Other birds are summer visitors and some stay to breed. Many others species pass through in spring and autumn on migration between the Tropics and the Arctic. They use the estuaries as vital staging posts, to rest and refuel.

Flock of knot

A commonly seen sight: *A pair of shelduck feeding*

The Dee Estuary is justifiably renowned for its birdlife but further west, Lavan Sands is equally special. The path between Llanfairfechan and Bangor takes you alongside a string of wetland nature reserves edging the coast. The reserves attract a good variety of birds throughout the year and, during the summer, lapwing and ringed plover breed here.

Seals and dolphins

Seals, porpoises and dolphins also enjoy the abundant food. There is a large population of grey seals on West Hoyle sandbank to the west of Hilbre Island and one or two are often seen bobbing in the water around Prestatyn or hauled out on the rocks below the Little Orme. Occasional dolphins and porpoises are also seen and have been known to swim up the River Dee as far as Queensferry.

Sand dunes and shingle

The shingle foreshore along many sections of the coast supports a range of unusual plants and animals. Shingle flowers have to be adapted to survive the dry, salty and windy conditions. Look for spiky sea holly or yellow horned poppy at Gronant, Kinmel Bay, Pensarn and Llanddulas.

During the summer, ringed plover and little terns nest on the shingle at Gronant. Ringed plover have also successfully nested at Pensarn beside a popular tourist beach! The little tern colony at Gronant is the only one in Wales. You may see these graceful birds diving for sand eels in the water or listen to the ceaseless chattering from the breeding colony.

The wide sand dunes at Gronant and Talacre dunes are alive with bird-song and colourful with wild flowers in the summer. Evening primrose, sea spurge, centaury, yellow-wort and a mass of marsh and pyramidal orchids flourish. The flowers attract many bees, butterflies and moths, including the distinctive red and black burnet moth. Further west remnant dunes remain at Kinmel Bay.

Skylarks sing as they soar high in the sky. In the dunes, you may see perky wheatears and stonechats whose call sounds like two pebbles being banged together. Delicate warblers flit around in the scrub. They are well camouflaged but you can't miss their melodious song. Kestrels hover above the dunes searching for prey and, at dawn or dusk, short-eared owls are out hunting.

Ringed plover

The rare natterjack toad and sand lizard have been reintroduced at Gronant Dunes and both now breed there.

Limestone cliffs and grassland

The limestone of the Great and Little Orme headland has a different but equally special flora and fauna. Wild flowers thrive on the thin limestone soils and in spring and summer, the grassland is carpeted with flowers such as thyme, dropwort, salad burnet, common rock rose and the rarer hoary rock rose and spiked speedwell. Maritime species such as sea campion, thrift and spring squill are also common. The flowers attract many butterflies and other insects. Over 24 butterflies species have been recorded, including the rare silver studded blue.

The steep cliffs above the sea are important nesting and roosting sites. Guillemots, razorbills, fulmars, kittiwakes and cormorants nest here whilst ravens, chough, peregrines and little owls inhabit the more remote cliffs.

Linnets, skylarks, stonechats and meadow pipits nest in the heathland or grassland. Wheatears arrive in the spring to nest among the rocks and walls and, in the winter, birds such as the snow bunting arrive from the Artic. Many other birds pass through on spring or autumn migration.

One of the most unusual sights on the Great Orme are the feral goats that roam freely across the grassland. These agile animals are an impressive sight with their white shaggy goats and curving horns.

Carneddau ponies

Watching you: *Feral goats on the Great Orme*

Mountains and Moorland

The wilder upland landscape of Conwy Mountain is spectacular in the summer when it is dominated by purple heather and yellow gorse. Many birds including skylarks, stonechats and pipits nest here. In July and August the bilberries are ripe, providing a tasty feast for wildlife and walkers!

You may hear the mew of buzzards circling overhead and the cronk of ravens as they fly past with steady flowing wing beats or acrobatically dive and roll. The endangered chough also thrives here, using its long curved beak to find insects in the grass and heath.

One of the most special sights are the hardy Carneddau wild ponies who graze the mountain throughout the year. These tough little ponies, with their long, shaggy manes, are thought to have lived here for at least 500 years.

Day sections:

1. Chester to Flint *13 miles/ 21 kilometres*

2a Flint to Talacre coast route *13½ miles/ 22 kilometres*
(Flint to Talacre woodland option *14½ miles/ 24 kilometres*)

3. Talacre to Pensarn, Abergele *13 miles/ 21 kilometres*

4. Pensarn to Llandudno *12½ miles/ 20 kilometres*

5. Llandudno to Conwy *8½ miles/ 14 kilometres*

6a. Conwy to Llanfairfechan coastal route *9 miles/ 14.5 kilometres*

6b. Conwy to Llanfairfechan upland route *11 miles/ 18 kilometres*

7. Llanfairfechan to Bangor *9½ miles/ 15.5 kilometres*

Llwybr Arfordir Cymru
Wales Coast Path

The
North Wales Coast
section of the
Wales Coast Path

View from Little Orme (Day Section 4)

Chester to Flint

Distance: *13miles/ 21 kilometres (including 2 ½ mile/ 3½ kilometres link route from Chester Station to Welsh border)*| **Start:** *Chester Station SJ413670*
Finish: Flint Castle SJ247733| **Maps:** *OS Landranger 117 Chester & Wrexham; and OS Explorer 266 Wirral and Chester + 265 Clwydian Range*

Outline: A flat but varied Day Section following the River Dee from the walled town of Chester, continuing along the river as it widens into the estuary, ending beside the dramatic ruin of Flint Castle

Follow the canal towpath through the city to reach the river. The route then follows Cycle Route 568 alongside the river to Queensferry. Here it crosses the river and then across riverside meadows to Wepre Riverside and Connah's Quay Dock, with their maritime scuplutures and artefacts. There is then 2½ miles/4 kilometres of pavement alongside the A548 to Oakenholt, before crossing Flint Marsh to end at Flint Castle.

Services: *Chester has plenty of accommodation, banks, post office, shops, pubs and bars, restaurants, cafés and takeaways. Roman Amphitheatre, City Walls, Cathedral, Grosvenor Museum. B&B at Oakenholt Farm, informal cafe at Connah's Quay Docks and other facilities in Connah's Quay town and Flint, train stations at Chester, Shotton and Flint, regular bus services. Chester TIC 0845 647 7868; www.visitchester.com.*

👁 **Don't miss:** Chester City – Medieval walls, Roman amphitheatre, cathedral| John Summers building and old wharves – reminders of the industrial and maritime past | Waders and wildfowl on Flint Marsh

▲ *Old wharves at Queensferry*

Chester

The historic city of Chester is an ideal place to begin your walk as the rise of the city is closely linked with the River Dee. Chester developed as a Roman port and its maritime importance continued through the Middle Ages until the Dee began to silt up. During the Civil War, small boats sailed up the river from Flint Castle to get supplies to the besieged city, which was a Royalist stronghold. Nowadays the city is very different but the canal and river remind of its maritime past.

The Shropshire Union Canal by Telford's Warehouse, Chester

The route: **Chester to Flint**

1 From the station entrance, carefully cross the road, pass the Queen Hotel on the left and then walk up **City Road**. Immediately after crossing over the canal, take steps down to the left and then turn right to walk along the canal towpath (refreshments available at several canal-side pubs along this stretch). Continue along the towpath, soon with the sandstone 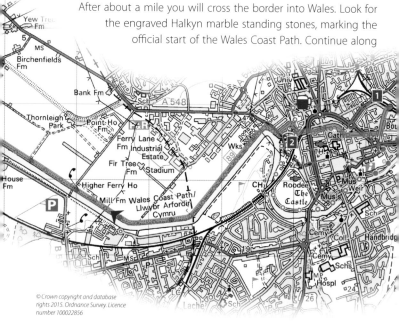 **City Walls** on your left and passing **Northgate Locks** on the right. Follow the canal as it bears right under a bridge then widening into a canal basin by **Telfords Warehouse** (Crane Wharf).

Follow the path alongside the water, walking between two sections of canal basin. Turn left and cross a small footbridge over the second canal, then follow path to leave the canal basin through a hole in the wall, emerging at a road junction. Cross the roads and walk ahead down **Catherine Street** to the main road, A548. Carefully cross the busy road then turn left and right a few metres later into **'The Cop'** recreation ground.

2 Follow the clear concrete path alongside the river. You are now on Cycle Route 568 that you will follow for 5½ miles/9 kilometres, all the way along the River Dee to Queensferry. Beware of cyclists as it is a popular route!

After about a mile you will cross the border into Wales. Look for the engraved Halkyn marble standing stones, marking the official start of the Wales Coast Path. Continue along

Along the riverbank: *The River Dee near Queensferry*

the riverside path passing the footbridge at **Higher Ferry**. (You can detour over the footbridge and left along the opposite bank to see sculptures and interpretation about the shipbuilding and other industries that developed at Saltney. There is also parking available behind Go Outdoors, for those wishing to walk the path without going into Chester.)

Until 1960 a ferryman used to carry passengers across the water to work in the aircraft factory and the shipyards, chainmakers and factories of Saltney. Further along, on the opposite bank look for the moorings of the Airbus barges that transport the massive A380 wings along the river to Mostyn for export to France.

3 When you reach the blue metal bridge, cross the road and turn left to cross the bridge. On the opposite bank turn right onto a small lane, signed Riverside Walk, then left by Bridge Villas onto a track. Go through a small metal gate beside a wooden one and, by a second wooden gate, turn right through a small kissing gate. Follow the narrow enclosed path, eventually going through another kissing gate to emerge onto the open marsh. Walk directly ahead on the raised bank with the river on the right, heading towards the cream railway bridge. Continue along the earth bank, briefly detouring inland around an inlet, until you reach the railway bridge. (Turn left here for Shotton Railway station.)

Edwardian grandeur: The John Summers offices, Shotton

The grand red-brick building on the opposite bank by the bridge is the former
👁 **John Summers steelworks offices**, *its Edwardian grandeur a testament
to the prosperity of the massive steelworks. John Summers senior, a Lancashire
clogger, bought a nail making machine at the Great Exhibition and began making nails to fasten iron strips onto the bottom of clogs. After his death, his sons
took over and expanded into North Wales, building the Shotton works in 1896.
By 1909 the company was the largest manufacturer of galvanized steel in the
country. Locals recall watching the coasters turning in the estuary to collect their
cargoes of sheet steel and coils of steel rope from the John Summers wharves.
The blue buildings on the opposite bank are the modern works, now run by Tata.*

*Hawarden Bridge opened in 1889 to take the railway across the river. It has
a swing section in the middle to allow shipping to pass, although this has been
not been operable since 1960.*

Go under the railway bridge, following the tarmac path. Where the tarmac
path goes inland, bear right onto a natural path that stays nearer the river,
walking with grazing marsh on the right. Follow this raised grassy path, once
old sea defences, as it winds round back to the tarmac path. Go through a
gate and turn right, signed **Connah's Quay Dock**. At path fork bear right

through black barriers and follow path to the car park at **Wepre Riverside**. Look for the **Kathleen and May sculpture**, representing the most famous sailing vessel that was built here. From here walk along the pavement beside the sea wall.

Old wooden wharves once lined the riverside here and railway sidings ran along the wharf, bringing bricks and coal to be loaded onto the sailing ships and steamers moored alongside.

Evoking the maritime past

Look for the sculptures, art and maritime artefacts dotted along the Flintshire section of the Coast Path. Some have been created in partnership with local communities and schools, others have more mysterious origins. Most notable are the stencils created in secret by Random, a local artist known as Flintshire's Banksy, depicting those who live and work along the Dee Estuary. These include a fisherman, merchant seaman, steelworker, collier and lifeboat captain.

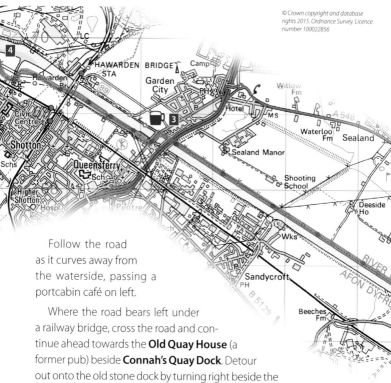

Follow the road as it curves away from the waterside, passing a portcabin café on left.

Where the road bears left under a railway bridge, cross the road and continue ahead towards the **Old Quay House** (a former pub) beside **Connah's Quay Dock**. Detour out onto the old stone dock by turning right beside the **Kathleen and May Heritage Centre** to enjoy the views of the river and imagine the bustling port in its heyday.

4 After exploring the old dock, take the path to the left of the pub, passing the old coach house and then turn right onto a tarmac path behind the pub. After about 300 metres the path turns left. Continue over the railway bridge and straight ahead along Rock Road to join B5129 on the outskirts of Connah's Quay. Turn right and walk along the pavement beside the road for just over ½mile/1 kilometre, passing Coleg Cambria on the left. Beyond the town, the road descends then rises to the the approach to a roundabout where the B road joins the A548. Carefully cross two roundabouts using the pedestrian ramps so that you are on the coastal side of the A road. At the second roundabout turn left into **Rockcliffe** and follow the pavement. Pass the power station entrance and carry straight ahead onto a path which soon joins the main road. Walk on the wide footpath on right-hand side of the A548 for 1¼ miles/2 kilometres.

5 Soon after passing The Yacht Inn on the right, turn right down a narrow driveway, just beyond some housing (look for Coast Path sign). Go through gate at the end and carefully cross the railway. Go through another gate and continue ahead on a clear path out onto **Flint Marsh,** passing the treatment works on the left.

The sandbanks and mudflats of the Dee Estuary are notorious for claiming lives, immortalised by Charles Kingsley in his poem, 'The Sands of the Dee'. An extract is included below.

"O Mary, go and call the cattle home,
And call the cattle home,
And call the cattle home,
    Across the sands of Dee!
The western wind was wild and dank with foam,
    And all alone went she.
The western tide crept up along the sand,
And o'er and o'er the sand,
And round and round the sand,
    As far as eye could see.
The rolling mist came down and hid the land-
    And never home came she."

Fishing boats at Connah's Quay

Just beyond the treatment works, turn half-left onto the marsh, following a meandering path that gradually bears right towards the estuary, walking towards a mound and small wooden footbridge. Continue across the marsh on a narrow natural path (can be boggy!) crossing ditches on wooden boardwalk. Continue walking with the estuary to the right, following path as it meanders inland, eventually walking alongside a hedge on the left.

Continue to the end of the marsh, then go through a gate onto a surfaced path. Turn right and follow path to the coast. Go through gates then turn left and follow wide tarmac path alongside the estuary, walking towards the ruin of Flint Castle. This area is a great place for watching 👁 **waders and wildfowl** especially in the winter.

Follow the path past the rugby pitch and lifeboat station then cross the car park heading towards the castle. Turn left and walk along the pavement, alongside a deep grassy ditch that was once the outer moat of the castle. This day section ends at the site of the outer gatehouse to the castle (tarmac path on the right leads to the main castle entrance).

For **Flint Station** or to walk into the town for shops and refreshments, turn left here, cross the road and walk along Castle Street. At the station, cross the railway footbridge to continue into town.

Curlews on the saltmarsh

A birdwatcher's paradise

The Dee Estuary is a rich feeding ground for thousands of birds

Flint Marsh is is a great place for bird watching, particularly in the winter when the resident birds are joined by thousands of waders and wildfowl seeking refuge from colder climes. When the tide is out you can see them feeding on the mudflats but high tide is also good for birdwatching as the birds are pushed up onto the saltmarsh.

Oystercatchers are very common. They're certainly the easiest to recognise — and the noisiest! Around 10% of the British population live here and you often see large groups on the saltmarsh at high tide or probing in the mud for cockles, when the tide is out. Other common species include curlew, tall waders with long curved beaks and a distinctive 'curl-ee' call and redshank, smaller and more active waders, easily identified by their bright red legs. There are egrets too, once only associated with hotter climes but now a familiar sight here.

Look for pairs of shelduck, larger than the other ducks with a large red beak and white, chestnut and black plumage. In winter large flocks of pintail and wigeon arrive. Black-tailed godwits also overwinter in large numbers.

More information: For details of the best birdwatchingsites and sightings: www.deeestuary.co.uk/

Old dock Connah's Quay

Docks and shipyards

Small ports, shipyards and industries developed along the Dee

The Dee has been used for transport for thousands of years. Chester was an important Roman and Medieval port but, as early as the 15th century, the silting of the river prevented large ships from reaching the city. In 1737, the River Dee New Cut, was built to solve the problem. This deep water channel followed the southern bank of the Dee from Chester to the hamlet of Golftyn, where a stone pier was built to shelter boats. The area around the pier developed into the port of Connah's Quay and other small quays were built along the river. The easy river transport encouraged the establishment of numerous industries, bringing employment and prosperity.

By the early 20th century, Connah's Quay was one of the largest and most important ports on the Dee Estuary. It's hard to imagine

The launch of the Kathleen and May

the river crowded with boats and barges delivering and collecting their cargoes, exporting coal, bricks, chemicals and fertilizers, and importing timber. In 1844 ships were leaving Connah's Quay for Barrow, Cardigan, Ireland, France, Germany, Nova Scotia and Norway. Tramways and railways linked the port with nearby ironworks and collieries. In 1862, the opening of the railway to Buckley meant their bricks and tiles could be exported across the world.

Crichton's shipyard, Saltney

Rope was essential for sailing ships and, in the early 19th century Bagillt, had the longest ropewalk in Britain. Rope was replaced by metal chains and, by 1872, Henry Woods Chain Works at Saltney was said to be, *'the largest and most complete in the kingdom for producing all descriptions of chains, cables and anchors and crane chains for collieries and lifting purposes'.*

Shipbuilding flourished too. Ferguson and Baird, initially at Flint and later Connah's Quay, were renowned for their wooden sailing ships. One of their best known vessels was the Lizzie May (later renamed the Kathleen and May),

the last remaining British wooden hull three-masted top sail schooner. She continued as a trading schooner until 1961 and is now moored in the Albert Dock.

After they closed in 1916, the yard was re-opened by J Crichton & Co, building metal ships until the mid 1930s.

Other small shipyards operated between the mid 19th and mid 20th century at Queensferry and Sandycroft, including Thomas Cram and Co who built the Royal Charter, a steam clipper. She was launched in 1855 but wrecked off Anglesey just four years later during severe storms on her return from Australia, with the loss of over 400 lives.

> *"The Kathleen and May is the UK's last working wooden topsail schooner, one of the few remaining links to the long-vanished trading fleets that used to sail Britain's waters."*
>
> National Historic Ships UK

Flint to Talacre

Distance: *13½ miles/ 22 kilometres or 14½ miles/ 25 kilometres with woodland option* | **Start:** *Flint Castle SJ247733* | **Finish:** *Talacre, Station Road SJ125848*
Maps: *OS Landranger 117 Chester & Wrexham + 116 Denbigh & Colwyn Bay; OS Explorer 265 Clwydian Range*

Outline: A delightful easy walk alongside the widening Dee Estuary, ending at Talacre with its wide beach and iconic lighthouse.

After exploring the castle, walk beside the estuary round Flint Point and along Bagillt Cop to the viewpoint at Bettisfield. The path continues along the coast to picturesque Greenfield Dock, with its pretty fishing boats, and on towards the larger Port of Mostyn. If time, take the inland route to enjoy the tumbling woodland waterfalls, then continue through Ffynnongroyw and along the old sea defences and beside saltmarsh to Point of Ayr and the beach at Talacre.

Services: *Flint has a bank, post office, shops, pubs, cafés and takeaways. Detour inland to cafe in Greenfield Valley Heritage Park and all facilities in Holywell. Café at Abakhan Mill and pub at Llannerch-y-mor, pubs and shop in Ffynnongroyw and restaurant and B&B at Llinegar Inn; pubs, cafe, shops at Talacre; good bus service along A548*

👁 **Don't miss: Flint Castle** – the first of Edward I's iron ring of Welsh castles | **Bettisfield viewpoint** – great views from this former colliery site | **Greenfield Dock** – pictureque dock that once served the mills of Greenfield Valley

▲ *Greenfield Dock*

Flint

At first glance, it's hard to imagine that this bustling little town has medieval origins. When King Edward I ordered the building of Flint Castle in 1277, he laid out an adjoining new town to support the castle and provide a commercial centre.

The medieval town was built on a regular grid pattern, modeled on the bastide towns of France. There were six parallel streets running north-east to south-west and one cross-route. The present Church Street was the principal thoroughfare, running south-west from the castle and all the key buildings in the town were built here. The castle, the market square (the area around the present Town Hall) and the church are all in a direct line.

In the 1700s an industrial area began to develop near the coast, with the port exporting coal from local collieries and lead from the newly opened smelter. The opening of the railway in 1844 and the building of alkali works in 1852 brought further growth and the town prospered, expanding well beyond the original medieval walls. First the grand Town Hall and then the church were rebuilt in this period, paid for by the local gentry and businessmen. Many of the buildings on Church Street and Trelawney Square date from this era of prosperity. Most look very different nowadays but older facades remain above the modern shop fronts.

High tides can still reach Flint Castle

The route: **Flint to Talacre**

1 From **Castle Dyke Street** in front of 👁 **Flint Castle**, walk up the clear path towards the castle and turn left just before the entrance. Descend the grass bank to a small car park beside woodland then take the path on the right between trees, walking past the castle on the right.

Bear right where the path forks (or detour left uphill to the viewpoint) walking alongside the coast, enjoying the wide views across the river and upstream, with the power station chimneys and Flintshire Bridge on the skyline. Continue on this natural path meandering through scrub woodland.

Continue straight across an access drive, onto a higher path along the woodland edge, soon walking with the estuary on the right again. Follow this path round the small headland and alongside a creek to the former **Flint Dock**.

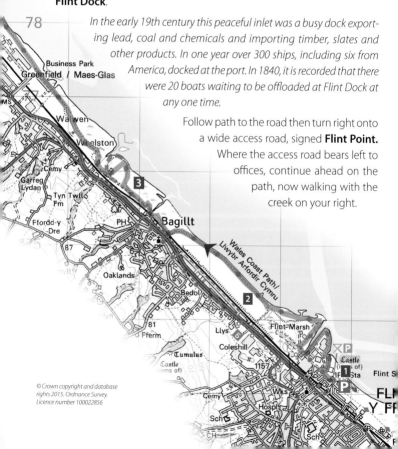

In the early 19th century this peaceful inlet was a busy dock export-
ing lead, coal and chemicals and importing timber, slates and
other products. In one year over 300 ships, including six from
America, docked at the port. In 1840, it is recorded that there
were 20 boats waiting to be offloaded at Flint Dock at
any one time.

Follow path to the road then turn right onto a wide access road, signed **Flint Point.** Where the access road bears left to offices, continue ahead on the path, now walking with the creek on your right.

© Crown copyright and database
rights 2015. Ordnance Survey.
Licence number 100022856

The remains of the massive Donjon Tower at Flint Castle

A military stronghold

An army of workers were needed to build a castle

Edward I chose the site of his first Welsh castle carefully, a rocky promontory on the marshes at an easy crossing of the Dee Estuary, easily accessible by both land and sea. Just 10 miles east lay Chester, the principal medieval port of north west England, a vital supply base for Edward's invasion. Across the water lay the Wirral with its plentiful supply of raw materials.

In charge of the work was Richard L'Engeneur from Chester, a leading military engineer who was an ancestor of the Duke of Westminster.

Thousands of drafted labourers were forcibly marched from many parts of England. The first task was to dig the defensive moats and foundations. By August 1277, there were over 2000 dykers at work, including many from the Fens and some from Holland.

By 1278 many dykers had moved onto Rhuddlan, the site of Edward's second castle, and most of the wages were spent on quarry workers. Much of the stone was quarried at Ness and shipped across the Dee on rafts. Over the coming years numerous stone masons worked to dress and lay the stones.

Building continued for over nine years. The total costs of the build was estimated to be £6791 – around £4.5million in today's terms!

More information: Open daily from 10.am until 4pm, free entry; www.cadw.gov.wales/daysout/flintcastle

At path fork, bear right out to **Flint Point** to enjoy the wide views, then follow the white path meandering through scrub, with the estuary to the right. Continue on this path as it bears left, slightly inland, and passing green huts on the right. Ignore a path joining from the left, continuing on main path bearing right and walking back towards the coast.

2 Just after the main path swings inland, turn right onto a narrower path and right again at a T junction. You are now on Panton Cop. Turn left and follow the narrow raised path along the top of the sea wall for 1 mile/1.5 kilometres, enjoying the wide views across the estuary to the Wirral and Hilbre Island.

'Cop' is a local word meaning the top of a sea bank. The sea wall was originally built in the 1800s, enclosing the marsh to create grazing land and providing land on which the railway was built in 1848.

The outlet of the Milwr Tunnel, 'The Holy'

Beware of the dragon: *The beacon at Bettisfield viewpoint is lit for celebrations*

Follow the path as it bends inland then bears right, running alongside the railway. Continue as it meanders across open ground. At the end of this path, go through a gate and walk across a parking area to **Station Gutter**, where a river outlet joins the estuary. A panel explains that this was once an important wharf. Cross the bridge over the gutter, signed to **Bettisfield**, and follow the pale surfaced path ahead, which runs along a small embankment. Continue along the clear path, walking towards the grassy hill ahead.

3 At a footpath junction at the bottom of the hill, turn right and follow the path round the edge of the saltmarsh. (Turning left then following the inland path right passes a car park and seating area.) Ignore the first kissing gate on the left, then follow the path through a second kissing gate. At a path fork beside a bench, take the left-hand fork and continue on path, gently climbing up the hill. Where the surfaced path ends turn left and walk across the grass to ☻**Bettisfield viewpoint** heading for the impressive metal dragon, which is one of a series of beacons along the coast.

The hill was a spoil heap from Bettisfield Colliery, one of the largest of the collieries along the Dee Estuary that worked the rich coal seams below the sea bed. The shafts were sunk in 1871 and, at its peak production in 1908, it employed 641 men. It closed in 1933, having been hit badly by strikes and the Depression.

Colourful fishing boats: Time to catch the tide at 'The Holy', Bettisfield

Detour: *to 'The Holy' or to avoid the climb to the viewpoint*
From the path junction by the bench, continue on the lower path above
the estuary and follow it round to the little fishing harbour, known as 'The
Holy'. To rejoin the official route, either retrace your steps to the summit
or follow the access road from the harbour back inland.

On the **official route** from **Bettisfield viewpoint** pass the beacon on your
left and follow the wide grassy path down the hillside, towards an old brick
building, which was the colliery engine house. At the bottom of the hill,
go through a gate and take right-hand path fork, signed **Milwr Tunnel**.
Continue ahead where the path joins a road by big boulders, ignoring the
access road that curves right. Go through a gap by a metal barrier along a
surfaced road. Follow the road through wasteland, crossing a bridge over
a gushing stream of clear water.

*This powerful stream of water is the outlet of the Milwr Tunnel, a 10 mile long
drainage tunnel, built in stages between 1857 and 1957 to drain the Halkyn
lead mines. It enabled deeper mining to continue productively into the 1950s.
It is known locally as 'The Holy' because the same source of water also feeds St
Winefride's Well at Holywell.*

Follow the concrete path that bears right, then turn left through another kissing gate, signed Coast Path, and continue along the surfaced path. Eventually go through a small metal gate and, with saltmarsh on your right, follow the clear path ahead for about a kilometre. Take the first turning right onto a wide tarmac track which hugs the coast. Follow as it bends round to the left along the coast until it reaches the car park at 👁 **Greenfield Dock**.

'The Legend of Winefride'

Legend tells that Caradog, a royal prince, cut off Winefride's head after she spurned his advances. Her uncle, St Beuno, miraculously restored her to life and a spring burst forth from the ground where her head fell. St Beuno prophesied that anyone who asked for Winefride's help at that spot would receive it. St Winefride's Well continues to be a site of pilgrimage today.

The dock is still used by fishing boats and by cocklers but was once a busy port, serving the copper mills of Greenfield Valley, and also bringing passengers from the Wirral and Liverpool to St Winefride's Well in nearby Holywell.

Detour: *To Basingwerk Abbey and Greenfield Valley*

Turn left away from the coast and walk along the pavement beside a minor road. At the junction with A548, carefully cross at the traffic lights and then turn left and, just before the Greenfield Valley car park, turn right up a track, emerging with the café and Basingwerk Abbey on left and the Visitor Centre ahead.

Basingwerk Abbey was founded in the 12th century. Its monks were Cistercian, known as 'white monks' due to the colour of their habits. The Abbey became very wealthy, owning grazing land for over 2000 sheep. The monks used the power of the fast flowing stream to grind corn and process the wool from their flocks. They started the market in Holywell in 1292, selling their own produce and collecting taxes from their merchants and farmers who came to sell their wares. The Abbey thrived for centuries but was closed following Henry VIII's Dissolution of the Monasteries in 1536.

The fast flowing water enabled Greenfield to be at the forefront of the Industrial Revolution in North Wales. At its peak water wheels powered around 20 factories. Copper works, cotton mills, paper mills and many other industries were drawn to the Valley, making Holywell the most important industrial town in North Wales in the 1800s.

View from Greenfield Dock

Evocative ruins: *The ruins of Basingwerk Abbey give an idea of its former importance*

To explore the valley further, take the tarmac path straight ahead, passing the Visitor Centre on the left and the Victorian School building on the right. Go through gates and bear slightly left, following the narrow road uphill. You will see ruined mills and a large mill pond to the right of the road. Retrace your steps back to **Greenfield Dock** to rejoin the Coast Path.

NB Check the tide times before walking the next section as it can flood at high tide by the grounded Duke of Lancaster ship.

4 Back on the **official route**, walk along the western side of the dock (at the far end is a panel and plaque relating to the maritime history). From the car park, go through a gate on the left and follow the natural path along a raised grassy embankment running parallel with the coast. (Just over a kilometre along the path an alternative high tide route is signed inland along a footpath, but the subsequent walk alongside the road is less pleasant than the coastal route so it is worth avoiding high tide if at possible.)

Continue along this raised path, walking towards the large ship now visible ahead. Eventually go through a gap beside a gate and follow path towards the ship.

The ship is the 'Duke of Lancaster', a former passenger ferry. It was once known locally as the 'fun ship', renowned for its discos. More recently graffiti artists from across the world have painted on its bows.

5 Follow the path left as it turns inland alongside a narrow creek (this is the section that can flood). Continue to the road. Turn right along the road, for a few metres, crossing a small bridge over the creek.

Detour: *To Abakhan Mill*

Turn right along the road a few metres to **Abakhan Mill,** a former lead smelting works, once

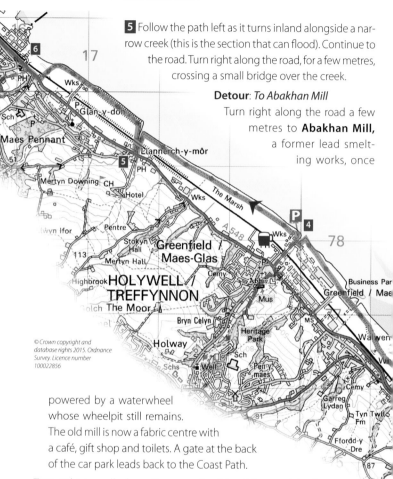

© Crown copyright and database rights 2015. Ordnance Survey. Licence number 100022856

powered by a waterwheel whose wheelpit still remains. The old mill is now a fabric centre with a café, gift shop and toilets. A gate at the back of the car park leads back to the Coast Path.

Turn right to walk along the opposite side of the creek back out towards the ship. Follow the clear path left up steps and then passing the old ship on the right. Continue on the path as it bears left, following the coastline once again.

6 Mostyn Port, still a working freight port and centre for the windfarm management, is visible ahead. As you approach the port and jetty, ignore a path left (this is the high tide route returning to the coast) and continue ahead towards the port. Go through a gap beside a large metal gate and follow the path left. Cross railway bridge and eventually go through a wooden gate to join the main road. Turn right along the pavement.

NB If you wish to avoid the next section along the busy main road, cross the road at the **Lletty Hotel** (closed at time of writing) and follow the directions at the end of the chapter (2b Official inland route on page 85). This alternative woodland route is slightly longer but far more enjoyable and well worth the detour if you have time.

2a: To continue on the official coastal route, carefully cross the main road at the traffic lights for Mostyn Port, and turn right to continue walking along the pavement on the opposite side of the road. At the traffic lights just past **Mostyn Lodge**, cross over the main road again and turn left to continue walking along the opposite pavement.

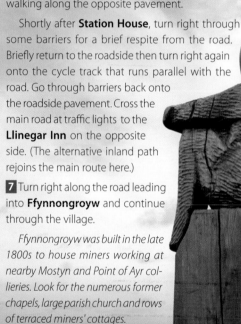

Shortly after **Station House**, turn right through some barriers for a brief respite from the road. Briefly return to the roadside then turn right again onto the cycle track that runs parallel with the road. Go through barriers back onto the roadside pavement. Cross the main road at traffic lights to the **Llinegar Inn** on the opposite side. (The alternative inland path rejoins the main route here.)

7 Turn right along the road leading into **Ffynnongroyw** and continue through the village.

Ffynnongroyw was built in the late 1800s to house miners working at nearby Mostyn and Point of Ayr collieries. Look for the numerous former chapels, large parish church and rows of terraced miners' cottages.

The Lookout by Mike Owens, Greenfield Dock

8 At the end of the village, turn right through a small metal gate, signed **Talacre.** Go through a second gate down to the main road. Turn left and cross at traffic lights, first stopping to look at the **mining memorial** on the grass verge. Turn right along opposite pavement, then left, signed 'Talacre', through a series of metal gates. Walk along the wide path on a raised bank above fields.

Go through a gate at the end of the raised path, bear left through a smaller gate onto a narrow path and then through a metal squeeze stile onto a road. Turn right and continue under the railway bridge. Take the tarmac path to the left of a large gate across the road. Cross an old access road and continue ahead on the clear tarmac path that curves right to return to the coast.

You are passing the site of the former colliery and may notice some of the old rail track along which coal was transported to the wharf.

Follow this clear path alongside the saltmarsh and creek, continuing as it curves inland. At the end of the tarmac path continue ahead to join a surfaced path along the sea wall.

Point of Ayr was the last deep coal mine in North Wales, closing in 1996. It was the major employer in the area for over 100 years,

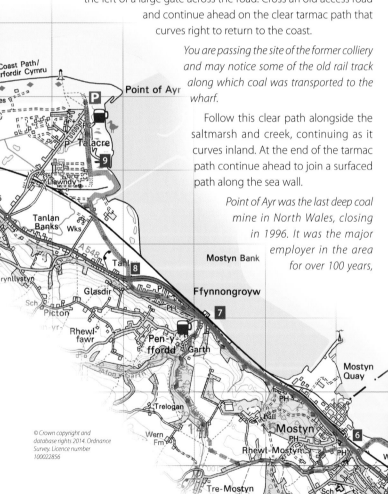

Stranded ship: *The graffitied hulk of the Duke of Lancaster ferry is a local landmark*

employing 839 men at its peak in 1959. Coal was exported to Ireland by ship from the wharf until 1959.

Detour: *To visit the RSPB bird hide that overlooks the estuary*
Turn right where the surfaced path begins and continue quietly to the wooden hide. High tide is the best time to visit when the rising tide forces the birds onto the saltmarsh.

9 For the **official coastal route,** continue on the raised path, signed 'Talacre', with the estuary on the right and the gas terminal on the left. At the end of this path, go through a gap between metal barriers to join **Station Road** at Talacre where this Day Section ends. Turn left down the road for refreshments and buses or, for the coast path, continue ahead (see next chapter).

2b: Official inland route: *Avoiding busy road past Mostyn*
At the **Lletty Hotel** cross the road and take the natural path (signed with blue bridlepath arrow) uphill into the woods from the far end of the car park. Continue uphill on this sunken woodland path then continue ahead on an access road for housing.

Where the access road forks, continue ahead, slightly uphill, passing houses on the left. Ignore footpath sign on right and continue up the track, slowly climbing. Go through the gate at the top and continue ahead,

Tumbling stream: *Ferns and mosses thrive along the stream above Ffynnongroyw*

passing a converted barn on right. Beyond the buildings, go through a metal gate and follow path down into woodland. Follow the path crossing a small footbridge and continue on the path along opposite side of the stream until you reach a wooden finger post. Take the narrower path right, signed **Ffynnongroyw**, now climbing through woodland, eventually walking with fields on the left and the wooded valley down to the right.

At a path fork bear left along the woodland edge, still slightly climbing and eventually going through a metal gate onto a road. Turn right along the road and follow for about ¾ mile/1 kilometre. At a road junction turn left on the road, signed **Tre-mostyn**, passing through a small road tunnel with a gatehouse perched above it (associated with the Mostyn estate).

Two hundred metres past a house on the right and a bridlepath on the left turn right through a wooden gate, signed Ffynnongroyw. Follow the natural path through woodland. Go through a gate into fields, then turn left and walk along the left-hand field edge. At the field corner, turn right and continue to a gate.

Go through gate into a field with a cross country course and turn right, now walking along the right-hand field edge. Follow down to a double gateway and turn right onto a wide track (can be muddy).

About 200 metres along the track, turn left through a gate into woodland and follow the wide path downhill. Continue over boardwalk through wet woodland. Ignore a narrow path down to the stream and keep following the main path ahead, walking with stream and gorge down on the left. At a path fork bear left on the lower path steadily descending down steps to **Garth Mill** buildings, which become visible behind the trees.

Turn right where the natural path joins a concrete path then walk down the side of the mill on a gravel path. Turn right past the mill, cross a footbridge over the stream and follow the drive to the road, beside the **Llinegar Inn** to rejoin the coastal route.

Miners' Memorial, Ffynnongroyw

Talacre to Pensarn

Distance: *13 miles/ 14½ kilometres* | **Start:** *Talacre SJ 125 848*
Finish: *Pensarn (station)SH 94678 7* | **Maps:** *OS Landranger 116 Denbigh & Colwyn Bay; OS Explorer 265 Clwydian Range + 264 Vale of Clwyd*

Outline: A refreshing walk along the beach and through the dunes, then seaside fun along the promenades of Prestatyn and Rhyl.

From Talacre, the first section is on sand along Talacre beach passing the famous lighthouse (there is tarmac path option through dunes, if pre-ferred) and then meandering on natural paths through Gronant Dunes to Barkby Beach at Prestatyn. From Barkby Beach the path follows the promenades through the seaside resorts of Prestyn and Rhyl, crosses the river mouth at Horton's Nose then continues along the seafront past Kimmel Bay all the way to Pensarn.

Services: *Shop, pub, café and public toilets in Talacre. Choice of accommodation and all facilities in Prestatyn and Rhyl; public toilets, information and refreshments at Rhyl Harbour; public toilets and kiosk at Kimnel Bay; refreshments and shops in Pensarn. Stations at Prestatyn, Rhyl and Pensarn*

👁 **Don't miss:** Talacre beach and lighthouse – long, open beach with wide views| **Gronant Dunes** - wildflowers and butterflies | **Rhyl Harbour** – pretty harbour with eyecatching modern lift bridge

▲ *Remnant dunes at Kimnel Bay*

Talacre

The wide sandy beaches at Talacre have long attracted holidaymakers. Numerous wooden chalets dotted the sand dunes of Talacre Warren and many Merseysiders have happy memories of childhood holidays spent there. They have now been replaced by more modern caravan parks but the beach and dunes have not lost their appeal.

Talacre, at the mouth of the Dee, has always been a treacherous point for shipping. The lighthouse was built in 1777 to mark the entrance to the estuary following the loss of two ships, their crew and cargo. It was taken out of use in 1883, replaced by the Dee light-ship, but remains one of Flintshire's most treasured landmarks. It even featured in a television advert for paint, although, at time of writing, it was in need of redecoration!

Talacre lighthouse built at the mouth of the Dee Estuary

Iconic view: *The lighthouse from the dunes*

The route: **Talacre to Pensarn**

1 From the top of **Station Road** continue ahead bearing right at the path fork to climb wooden boardwalk up to a wooden viewing platform. Go down steps and walk to the beach heading to a wide gap in the dunes. Go through this gap onto the beach and then turn left along the beach.

Alternative route: *Avoiding the beach*

If you do not wish to walk on sand or at very high water, turn left through a gate at the end of Station Road onto the surfaced cycle route and follow this clear path through the dunes and **Presthaven Sands Caravan Park** to rejoin the main path at the entrance to the caravan park.

On the **official route**, continue along the beach for about 1¼ miles/2 kilometres, soon passing Talacre Lighthouse on the right. Ignore signed paths to **Presthaven Sands** at gaps in the dunes. At the end of the beach continue ahead on a wide sandy path, now with saltmarsh on the right. Pass some small lagoons on the right and continue as the path narrows. Follow this path ahead until it emerges beside a small roundabout near the entrance to the caravan park. Follow the pavement round the roundabout to the main entrance.

2 Where the road bends left at the entrance, continue ahead through a small gate onto a tarmac path. After few metres, turn right at a wooden finger post, signed **Viewing platform**. Follow the narrow path through the reed-bed, crossing a footbridge and heading out to the coast. Where the path joins a wider grassy path in front of a large lagoon, turn left and walk with the lagoon on the right. Continue ahead on this natural path, ignoring path to Viewpoint platform on right by the little tern panel.

Detour: *To the viewing platform and tern colony*
Turn right at the waymarker to the viewing platform. From here, during late spring and early summer, it is well worth detouring right along the shingle at the top of the beach to visit the little tern colony. The nesting area is fenced off and wardened to avoid disturbance. (Please follow the guidance given.)

Along the dunes: *The meandering path leads along the ridge of the outer dunes at Gronant*

Continue ahead on natural path through 👁 **Gronant Dunes** ignoring paths left or right. (At low tide, you can cut down to the right and walk along the beach but please check the tide timetable as some of the foreshore is covered at high tide.) Eventually the dune path emerges on top of the dunes, now walking just above the coast. Follow this meandering waymarked path, mainly following the outer ridge of the dunes with great views out to sea. Gradually the dunes narrow and you will see golf links down on the left. Follow the path alongside the golf course, eventually walking on boardwalk. Pass another viewing platform on the right but continue ahead along the edge of golf course until you reach a small car park at **Barkby Beach**. Turn right and walk along the pavement to the promenade. Turn left here and walk along the promenade into Prestatyn.

Dechrau a Diwedd, the eye catching sculpture on Prestatyn seafront, marks the point at which Offa's Dyke National Trail reaches the coast in North Wales. It runs for 170 miles from Chepstow on the South Wales coast. You can circumnavigate Wales by walking both Offa's Dyke and the Wales Coast Path!

3 Turn left here and follow the promenade into **Prestatyn**. Continue walking along the promenade for 4½ miles/7 kilometres through the bustling seaside

resorts of Prestatyn and then **Rhyl**, where there are plenty of opportunties for refreshment stops.

Both resorts developed in the 1800s when sea bathing first became fashionable. From 1827, paddle steamers brought passengers from Liverpool and the industrial Lancashire towns to Rhyl. It grew rapidly from a little village of 300 to a fashionable resort with grand hotels and its own pier. The opening of the Chester to Holyhead Railway in 1848, with stations at Prestatyn and Rhyl, brought more

Little tern colony

The colony on the shingle at Gronant is the largest in Wales. Numbers have increased from 15 breeding pairs in 1975 to 136 pairs in 2014. The terns spend winter in Senegal but return in late spring to breed. You will hear the terns from some distance and notice the adults diving into the sea for fish. The chicks hatch from late June. Feeding them is an intense and demanding job. They fly just 16 days after hatching, increasing their body weight by up to 20% per day!

Dechrau a Diwedd: *'The beginning and the end' sculpture on Prestatyn sea front*

visitors and from further afield. Prestatyn only had a population of 500 before the railway opened , but then grew rapidly. Visitors flocked to the town drawn by its healthy reputation, with adverts boasting 'air being like wine and honey' and 'abundant sunshine ideal for arthritis and nervous disorders'.

4 At the end of Rhyl promenade, continue walking along the pavement with **Rhyl Harbour** on the right. Turn right and walk across the modern white footbridge, which can lift to allow boats to pass underneath. Bear left towards the the wooden-clad **Harbour Café and Bike-hub** then walk ahead passing the side of the building on the left. Follow a tarmac path past the boatyard and continue on this path back to the coast. Bear left and continue on this concrete path along the coast.

Look for the rows of wind turbines out at sea. North Hoyle, situated 4-5 miles off-shore between Rhyl and Prestatyn, was the UK's first large-scale offshore wind farm, operational since 2004. It comprises 30 turbines and produces enough energy to power up to 40,000 homes. Rhyl Flats, five miles off the coast between Abergele and Rhos-on Sea, was developed next. Its 25 turbines can potentially power up to 61,000 homes every year. The latest addition is Gwynt y Môr, which will be the second largest offshore wind farm in the world. When fully operational its 160 turbines will be capable of powering 400,000 homes.

Pyramidal orchids and burnet moth

Sand dune sanctuary

Flowers, animals and birds thrive in the dunes

Sand dunes once formed a continuous 4 mile ridge from Talacre to Rhyl but have been worn away by visitors and development. Many plants and animals depend on the dunes for survival so those that remain are really important habitats.

Sand dunes are constantly on the move as the wind blows the sand from one area to another. Marram grass grows along the seaward edge and has strong underground stems that trap the sand and help to build the dunes. Gradually other plants like sea holly get established but life is tough for these pioneer plants that need to conserve water. The leaves of the marram grass are rolled inwards and the prickly leaves of sea holly are waxy to reduce water loss.

Skylarks nest in the dunes between April and August. Male skylarks hover high in the air, singing loudly for several minutes proclaiming their territory in spring. More elusive residents are the rare natterjack toads and sand lizards. Natterjacks crawl rather than jump and dig burrows in the soft sand, emerging at night to feed on insects.

In June and July the dunes are full of colour with swathes of pyramidal orchids, pretty pink centuary, yellowort and the distinctive greenish-yellow spurges. Colourful butterflies and moths are drawn to the wealth of flowers and grasses.

More information: http://flintshire.audio-guide.co.uk/5-talacre/

Friend or foe?: *North Hoyle was the first of several wind farms along the North Wales Coast*

The route now hugs the coast on this concrete path for 3 miles/ 5 kilometres to the end of this day section. Pass the refreshment kiosk at Kinmel Bay and continue along the path, passing **Kinmel Dunes Nature Reserve** on the left and with shingle and pockets of remnant dune on the right.

Look for clumps of spiky sea holly on the shingle. In summer, listen for skylarks and look for perky wheatears perching on the sea wall and fence posts or flitting to catch insects.

Continue past housing and the **Golden Sands Caravan Park** on the left. Where there is a choice of paths take the upper, narrower path for pedestrians as it gives better views out to sea. Continue along the coast, eventually walking with the railway line on the left and follow to the minor road just beyond **Pensarn Station** where this day section ends. Turn left at the road junction to find shops or continue ahead to follow the Coast Path.

© Crown copyright and database rights 2015. Ordnance Survey. Licence number 100022856

Pensarn to Llandudno

Distance: *12½ miles/ 20 kilometres* | **Start:** *Pensarn Station SH 986747* **Finish:** *Llandudno Pier SH 783829* | **Maps:** *OS Landranger 116 Denbigh and Colwyn Bay; and OS Explorer 264 Vale of Clwyd + OL 17 Snowdonia*

Outline: An easy walk on concrete paths and promenades with wide views out to sea, and a delightful grassy section over the Little Orme.

From Pensarn the route follows the surfaced cycleway past Towyn and Llanddulas to Colwyn Bay, which hugs the coast and is quiet and peaceful. It then continues along Colwyn Bay promenade and on to Rhos on Sea before climbing on grassy paths up to the Little Orme for magnificent views along the coast then descending to finish with a walk along the broad, sweeping promenade of Llandudno.

Services: *Café and toilets on promenade at Pensarn. Plenty of cafes, pubs, takeaways, shops and accommodation at Colwyn Bay and Rhos-on-Sea. All facilities in the large seaside town of Llandudno. Railway stations at Pensarn, Colwyn Bay and Llandudno. Tourist Information Centre in Llandudno .*

Don't miss: **St Trillo's Chapel, Rhos on Sea** – diminutive chapel on the sea front | **The Little Orme** – a limestone headland with wonderful views | **Llandudno Promenade** – elegant Victorian seaside resort

▲ *Cyclists enjoying the views at Llanddulas*

Pensarn and Abergele

Pensarn is a small seaside resort, linked to the town of Abergele to the south. Abergele has a long history. Iron age hillforts were built on the hill tops behind the town, it was a Roman trading town, site of an important Celtic monastery and a medieval marketplace. In contrast Pensarn is much younger, a traditional resort with sandy beach, promenade, amusements and cafes. Its name means 'end of the causeway' and it developed along a causeway that was built to cross Morfa Rhuddlan — the marshy area around the mouth of the river.

Breakwaters on Llanddulas beach with wind turbines out at sea

The route: **Pensarn to Llandudno**

1 Cross the minor road by **Pensarn Station** and follow a red tarmac path along the coast, passing a play area and fitness machines and a café on the left. Continue along the coast on this clear red path with shingle and maritime grassland on the right.

Ringed Plover have nested on the shingle, successfully raising 4 chicks in 2014, despite the closeness to the busy beach and coast path. The numbers of ringed plovers in the UK are falling so it is satisfying to see them here. The nesting areas may be fenced off. Please take care not to disturb them and ensure dogs are on leads. Many flowers thrive on the thin soils too including kidney vetch, white campion and birds foot trefoil.

The **official path** follows the cycleway but you may prefer to walk along the more natural shingle and grassy path nearer the beach, running parallel to the cycle track.

Look for Gwrych Castle high on the hillside to the left. Appearances can be deceptive as it was not built for defence. It is a Victorian Gothic structure, built between 1812 and 1822 on the site of an earlier Elizabethan house. It was the first Gothic folly to be built in Europe, commisioned by wealthy industrialist Lloyd Hesketh Bamford-Hesketh.

Pass a caravan park on the left then at **Tŷ Crwn**, go through a gap by a gate and, where the lane turns left, continue ahead along the coast on a narrower path. Continue on this path past the **Beachcomber pub** and another caravan park.

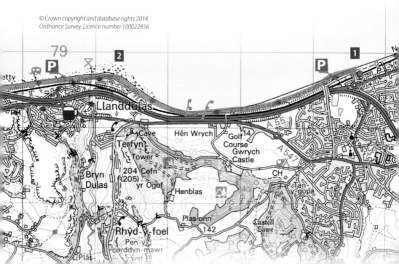

© Crown copyright and database rights 2014.
Ordnance Survey. Licence number 100022856

Determined birds: *Ringed plover nest at Pensarn, despite the holidaymakers*

Out to the right an unusual honeycomb worm reef carpets the lower shore. The hummocks are made up of countless tubes built by the honeycomb worm. When the reef is covered by the tide the worms poke their heads out of their tubes and use their tentacles to feed on tiny sea creatures.

Unusual maritime plants thrive on the shingle. Look for large clumps of spiky sea holly, the yellow-horned poppy and the tall, bright yellow evening primrose.

2 Soon after the caravan park the path becomes more sheltered and peaceful with wide views out to sea. As you near Llanddulas the path passes alongside a river, the Afon Dulas, on its way to the sea. Cross the river on a footbridge and continue ahead on the clear path, passing a road and tall railway bridge on the left.

Continue along the cycleway alongside the shingle beach at Llanddulas and then climbing a little above the coast for another 2½ miles/4 kilometres until you reach a road and the promenade at **Colwyn Bay**.

Look for the jetty where limestone quarried from south of the A55 is loaded onto ships for transport around the British Isles and Europe. The limestone is moved on a conveyor belt from the quarry to the jetty. The treacherous sea has wrecked two ships loaded with stone. One was wrecked off the Llŷn in 2011 and a much bigger vessel was wrecked at the jetty in a severe storm in 2012.

Bathing huts, Llandudno

Sun and sand

'Oh we do love to be beside the seaside'

Visitors have been enjoying the North Wales coast for 200 years. Doctors first highlighted the health benefits of sea bathing in the mid18th century and it soon became fashionable for the upper classes to visit the seaside to bathe and breathe the sea air. Three full immersions per day were recommended and reputedly cured numerous ailments from depression to tuberculosis. Bathing machines were introduced to allow swimming with decorum and these continued to be used into the 20th century.

Some resorts owe their early development to the paddle steamers that brought visitors on day trips from Merseyside and Lancashire. The first regular steam packet service began in 1821, ferrying passengers between Liverpool and Bagillt, but the service was soon extended to the Menai Straits and Beaumaris. In 1827 the terminus was moved to Rhyl, which had been little more than a few scattered houses at the mouth

On board the St Tudno paddle steamer, 1920s

of the River Clwyd but soon grew to become a popular resort.

For the wealthy, it was the combination of dramatic mountain scenery and picturesque coast that gave North Wales a special appeal. They were no longer able to undertake their 'Grand Tours' in Europe due to the instability following the French Revolution and were looking for alternatives. Some resorts attracted royalty and prime ministers, which further increased their allure. Gladstone favoured Penmaenmawr but also visited Llandudno, as did Disraeli, Lloyd George and Churchill. Edward, the Prince of Wales visited Llandudno in 1867 and 1880 and a string of European royalty also stayed there, including the Queen of Romania.

Edwardian fun at Prestatyn

The golden era for steamers was before the Great War, with over 300,000 passengers each summer season. The steamer services thrived as paid holidays, half day Saturdays, and an increased standard of living enabled the working classes to enjoy the seaside too.

> *"I can only say that I am delighted with this place, and indisposed and delicate as I am, I do not believe there is another place so good in the country."*
>
> Parry's Railway Companion from Chester to Holyhead, 1848 (referring to Prestatyn)

A surveyor visiting Llandudno in 1846 could see its potential, writing, 'What a charming watering place this would make.' Lord Mostyn was quick to agree and ten years later it was described as a 'salubrious and picturesque bathing place' with accommodation for thousands of visitors.

The North Wales coast railway line, which opened in 1848, made visits to the seaside available to an even wider audience and encouraged further growth of the resorts. At first the steamers and trains worked side by side and there was even an out by steamer, back by rail option for day trippers. Over time, rail took over and the steamer services reduced.

The heyday of the Victorian resorts has passed but the North Wales coast has not lost its appeal to visitors.

More information: Llandudno Museum has exhibitions about the development of the resort 01492 876517 www.llandudnomuseum.co.uk/

Many flowers grow on limestone grassland. Even the pockets of grassland alongside the cycle path are carpeted in flowers during the summer months, including orchids, purple knapweed and tall teasels.

3 At the end of the cycleway where a road comes under a bridge on the left, go through a gap by a small gate and walk along the promenade on the righthand side of the road. Continue along the promenade into Colwyn Bay, passing Porth Eirias watersports centre and restaurant on the right and a park on the left (you can walk through the park if you prefer to get away from the road) and then continue past the derelict Victoria Pier.

Victoria Pier was opened in 1900 and was a grand affair, including a 2500 seat pavilion to entertain the visitors who were flocking to the

resort. The pier has been ill-fated, seriously damaged by fires on three occasions, but was rebuilt each time. It is now closed and in very poor condition. Its future is uncertain.

Detour: *To Colwyn Bay Station and town centre*
To reach the town centre which has a good choice of shops, cafes and other facilities, cross the road and turn left to walk up the road to the station. Cross in front of the station and you will see the main shopping area ahead.

Follow the promenade around the sweeping bay into **Rhos on Sea,** a small seaside town with a peaceful atmosphere. There's plenty of choice of cafés, ice-cream parlours and shops and a small harbour and sandy beach.

Decaying grandeur: *Victoria Pier is a shadow of its former self*

Just beyond shops, café and kayak hire on a small headland on the right, bear right to keep as close to the coast as possible, walking along the lower promenade. Follow the promenade past 👁 **St Trillo's Chapel**, walking towards the Little Orme which is visible ahead.

Look for fossils in the massive limestone sea defence boulders on the right.

Go through **Penrhyn Bay** passing Penrhyn Bay Golf Course on the left and keep following the promenade towards the Little Orme.

At the end of the promenade, you have two options.

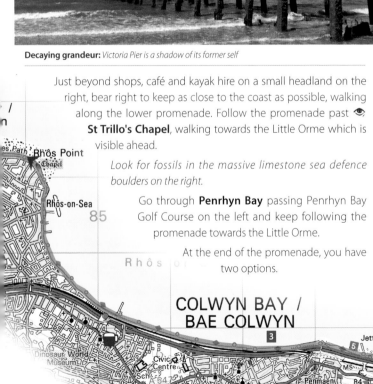

Panoramic views: *Looking out to sea from the top of the Little Orme*

Low tide route: Turn right down steps onto the shore, then turn left and walk along the beach towards the **Little Orme** (signed North Wales Path) with houses above on the left. Just after the last house turn left up steps. At the top of the steps turn right following the Wales Coast Path waymarker onto Penrhyn Beach East. Walk along the road through housing, ignoring a concrete path to the beach on the right.

4 On the **official route,** at the end of the promenade carry on along **Glan-y- Mor Road** then turn right onto **Beach Drive** past housing. At T junction turn right onto **Penrhyn Beach East** and continue through housing.

Where road bends left (becoming Penrhyn Beach West) continue ahead to the end of cul de sac and climb steps up to the left onto 👁 **the Little Orme**. Join a tarmac path by a Little Orme information panel, then turn right, now walking with the coast on the right. Follow clear path along the lower part of the Little Orme, continuing where it turns into a stony path.

Detour: *To the clifftop to overlook Angel Bay, a pretty little cove*
Grey seals are often seen hauled out on the beach at Angel Bay or bobbing in the water. January is a particularly good time to see them as mothers are sometimes resting on the shingle with their young pups.

Turn left by a wooden fingerpost, climbing steeply uphill on a clear grassy path, following the direction of the arrow.

Maritime flowers thrive on the thin cliff-top soils, including tufts of thrift with its distinctive pink flowers. Limestone-loving flowers such as birdsfoot trefoil and rockrose are also common on the grassy hillsides.

Go through kissing gate at top of hill and turn left along waymarked path (good views to right) passing the base of winding machinery from quarrying.

Saint Trillo's chapel

St Trillo's chapel, on the promenade at Rhos-on-Sea, is thought to be the smallest chapel in Britain with just six seats. It stands on the site of the cell built by St Trillo, a sixth century saint, probably chosen because of the spring that supplies fresh water. The simple altar of the present stone chapel stands above the spring, which was used for local baptisms for centuries. Take time to savour the tranquility of this peaceful chapel.

A rocky nest: *Fulmars nest on the cliffs*

The Little Orme has been used by man for thousands of years. Human bones dated as over 5000 years old were found here. In Tudor times, the first printing press in Wales was established in a cave to print Roman Catholic texts, away from persecution. More recently the limestone was quarried in the late 19th and early 20th centuries and a Coastal Artillery Training Camp was established here during the Second World War.

Follow natural grassy path along left-hand side of the hill. At a waymarker post, turn right uphill following the clear path. At the top of the hill, continue on the path as it bears right. Follow this clearly waymarked path, bearing left and keeping the fence on the left.

To the left are superb views across the Conwy Valley with the Carneddau and other Snowdonian mountains in the background.

Follow waymarkers, bear slightly left at path fork (waymarked). Go through a kissing gate on the left into **Rhiwledyn Nature Reserve** and follow natural path down the left-hand edge of the nature reserve

5 Go through a wooden kissing gate onto a busy road. Turn right and walk along the pavement until it joins ☜ **Llandudno promenade**. Follow the sweeping promenade along Llandudno sea front all the way to the pier where this day section ends.

Detour left into the town at any point along the promenade for shops, accommodation, refreshments, art gallery and tourist information.

Trams used to run along the wide promenade, providing a regular service between the town and Colwyn Bay from 1908 until the 1950s.

Walking along the promenade, edged by elegant white hotels, it is hard to imagine that, in the 1830s there were plans to develop the area as a port for exporting coal to Ireland instead of a seaside resort. A jetty was built in 1857 as the first part of the proposed harbour but a severe storm in 1876 washed it away and the plans were abandoned.

In 1877 the jetty was replaced by the wrought iron Victorian pier. It was built in stages and is now the longest pier in Wales. It had a bandstand at the seaward end and a grand pavilion at the shore end, which was renowned for its concerts. Famous performers in the 20th century included conductor Sir Malcolm Sergeant, comedian Ted Ray, George Formby, Petula Clark, and Cliff Richard. Paddle steamers brought passengers from Liverpool and ran pleasure trips along the Welsh coast. During the summer of 2015 two historic ships, the Waverley, which is the world's last sea-going paddle steamer, and the 'MV Balmoral', have made occasional sailings along the North Wales Coast, including calling at Llandudno pier. It is hoped that regular sailings from the pier might run again.

Llandudno from North Shore

Llandudno to Conwy

Distance: *8½ miles/ 14 kilometres* | **Start:** *Llandudno Pier SH 783829*
Finish: *Conwy riverside SH 783776* | **Maps:** *OS Landranger 116 Snowdonia; and Outdoor Leisure 17 Snowdonia*

Outline: Refreshing walking around the Great Orme and along the coast through Deganwy to Conwy, with magnificent views at all times.

From Llandudno Pier, the official route follows the pavement of Marine Drive around the Great Orme or you can clamber up grassy paths over the Orme and rejoin the route on West Shore. (Another option would be to spend an extra day in Llandudno to enable you to fully explore the Great Orme and enjoy the town.) From West Shore the path follows the water front along the estuary through Deganwy, eventually crossing beside Telford's iconic suspension bridge to reach Conwy.

Services: *Walkers are very well provided for on this section with all facilities in Llandudno and Conwy, cafés on Marine Drive and West Shore, pubs, shops, cafés and accommodation in Deganwy. Tourist information centres in Llandudno and Conwy. Train stations in Llandudno, Deganwy and Conwy*

👁 **Don't miss:** **Llandudno pier** – elegant Victorian pier that reminds of the age of paddle steamers and traditional entertainments| **The Great Orme** – magnificent limestone headland with panoramic views | **Conwy Estuary** – watching boats on the water with superb views to Conwy and Snowdonia

▲ *Llandudno Pier with the Little Orme in the background*

Llandudno

Elegant Llandudno was one of the most fashionable Victorian seaside resorts, known as the Queen of the Welsh Resorts. It was developed by the Mostyn family in the 1840s, designed to satisfy the leisure needs of Victorian society. Most of the early visitors came by paddle steamer but the opening of a branch line in 1858, linking the town with the Chester to Holyhead Railway brought thousands more.

By 1859 it had its own medical guide for visitors. The author, Dr JM Coley wrote that invalids and convalescents would find *"no locality uniting more charmingly a mild seaside residence with mountain scenery."*

The famous pier was the first of many Victorian attractions that all remain popular today. In 1887, Lord Mostyn closed Happy Valley quarry and gave the area to the town as a park to commemorate Queen Victoria's 50th jubilee, creating Happy Valley Gardens. Its attractions included a camera obscura and an open air theatre. The Great Orme Tramway, which climbs one mile to the summit, opened in 1902.

The resort has moved with the times and continues to thrive. A cable car up the Great Orme opened in 1969, the longest aerial cabin lift in the UK, and a dry ski slope and toboggan run built on part of Happy Valley.

Llandudno, an elegant Victorian seaside resort

The route: **Llandudno to Conwy**

1 With the entrance to 👁**Llandudno Pier** on your right walk along the pavement, passing the entrance to **Happy Valley Gardens** on left. Pass the toll house onto **Marine Drive** and continue walking along the pavement with the sea on your right. Just beyond the toll house look back for a fine view of the bay with the pier in the foreground and the headland of the Little Orme beyond.

Marine Drive was completed in 1878 as a carriage drive for the increasing numbers of visitors. Before this visitors had to use a dangerous path. Prime Minister William Gladstone walked it in 1868 and complained it was so bad that he had to be blindfolded to be led along some of the worst sections! Ratepayers money was used to erect railings along the most dangerous sections but, in 1872, the Great Orme's Head Marine Drive Company proposed the buidling of the new toll road, at a cost of £14000. It opened in 1878, charging pedestrians 1d, cyclists 2d, saddle horses 3d and carriages 6d per horse.

Sweeping bay: *Superb views of Llandudno Bay from the Great Orme*

The **official route** follows the pavement of **Marine Drive** for approximately six kilometres, circumnavigating the 👁 **Great Orme.** (An alternative route over the Great Orme is described overleaf.) To follow the offical route, walk along the pavement of Marine Drive continuing as it gradually climbs, ignoring the road to left that leads up the Orme.

Pass the entrance to the **Lighthouse Bed and Breakfast** on the right and, soon after, the **Rest and Be Thankful Cafe** (you will realise it is well-named if you are climbing against the prevailing wind!).

The lighthouse built on the cliffs 300' above sea level came into operation in 1862. Its powerful light that could be seen from 24 miles away guiding ships through the treacherous waters until 1985. The lighthouse was sold and now provides bed and breakfast accommodation in a truey unique setting.

Follow Marine Drive as it curves round the headland, enjoying magnificent views along the North Wales coast.

The land below is called the gunsite as it was used by the Royal Artillery School during the Second World War.

Continue round Marine Drive, now gradually descending. At the end of Marine Drive, go through a kissing gate beside a cattle grid and continue on the pavement towards Llandudno's **West Shore.**

Spectacular views: *Looking along the North Wales coast from the summit of the Great Orme*

Alternative route: *Via the Great Orme summit (numbered 2-5)*

If you prefer to get away from the road and climb the Orme itself you can follow grassy paths to the summit and zig-zag down the other side to rejoin the main path. This involves a steep climb but the magnificent views and colourful wildflowers more than compensate.

2 After rounding the first headland, just after the steep cliffs on the left give way to grassland, cross the road to take narrow, natural path on left, waymarked with Great Orme razorbill marker. Climb up steps and follow the narrow grassy path that winds up the hillside, climbing quite steeply.

In spring and summer the limestone grassland is dotted with wildflowers, the deep pink flowers of bloody cranesbill, yellow flowered rockrose and birds foot trefoil, white bladder campion, and meadowsweet with its clusters of tiny cream flowers.

At a path T junction, turn right and follow the yellow arrow as the path winds left uphill. Eventually, go through a wooden kissing gate onto a clear sunken path between two fields. Ignore the first path on the right to a white cottage, continuing on the waymarked path ahead.

Go through a wooden kissing gate then turn right, down to a gate in front of the white cottage. Go through the gate, following the permissive path (marked with a white arrow), passing the cottage and then farm buildings on the left, continuing along clear path between fields. Go through another wooden kissing gate. Pass **Powell's Well** on the left and go through another wooden kissing gate, following the clear path until it meets the road opposite the church.

Great Orme goats

*One of the more unusual sights on the 👁 **Great Orme** are the agile Kashmiri goats that graze freely across the headland. The original pair of goats was given to Lord Mostyn by Queen Victoria. The herd was released on the Orme around 1900 and have been roaming wild ever since. They feed on bramble, gorse and hawthorn which helps to keep the grassland open and allows wild flowers to flourish.*

Traditional travel: *A scenic ride on the Great Orme tramway*

Saint Tudno was an early Christian saint who established the first church on the Great Orme in the 6th century. He may have lived in a cave on the Orme. The present church was built in the 12th century and extended in the 15th century when it was the main place of worship for the scattered community. Following serious storm damage to the roof in 1839, it was decided to build a new church nearer the centre of the village (before Llandudno had developed into a town). The old church was neglected for some years until a local benefactor funded the repairs and it re-opened in 1855.

3 Turn left and walk alongside the road, passing the large cemetery on the right. Just beyond the cemetery, take the grassy path on the right, signed to '**the Summit**'. Climb steeply uphill toward the summit, then either cross under the cable car to detour to the triangulation point or turn right in front of cable car buildings and follow the path round to the summit café, car park and **Visitor Centre**.

The **Visitor Centre** (open from Easter to October) has informative displays about the Great Orme and its wildlife. There are leaflets and an audio trail to help you explore.

Leave the car park by the access road and walk downhill on grassy path on right-hand side of road. Pass a path to an **old quarry** on the right.

Razorbills gather on cliff edges

Birds and butterflies

Wildlife thrives on the cliffs and springy turf of the Orme

The Great Orme is designated as a Site of Special Scientific Interest in recognition of its national importance in terms of its geology and wildlife. Sea cliffs, limestone grassland, heathland and woodland all support different plants and animals.

In total 431 species of plants have been recorded here, including many rare and unusual species. In late spring and summer the springy turf of the limestone grassland is dotted with colourful wild flowers.

Wild thyme, carpets of yellow rock rose, birdsfoot trefoil and harebells are common. Coastal flowers also thrive so look for the delicate flowers of spring squill and clumps of pink thrift. There are also pockets of deeper soils where heathland plants like bell heather and gorse grow.

Numerous insects are drawn to the wild flowers, including twenty-one species of butterfly.

Hundreds of seabirds nest on narrow ledges on the undisturbed steep cliffs. The razorbill, with its distinctive thick blunt beak, is the symbol of the Great Orme Country Park. Kittiwakes, fulmars, cormorants and guillemots are also common and often seen flying to and from the cliffs or on the water below.

More information: Visit the summit visitor centre or online: **www.conwy.gov.uk/greatorme**

Perfect picnic spot: *Enjoying the views from the Great Orme*

4 Just beyond the quarry take path on right, signed **'to Town'**. Follow this natural path round the back of the old quarry, then bear left at path fork, following the razorbill waymarker. Follow the natural meandering path over the thin grassland, which is interspersed with limestone boulders and crags and strewn with flowers in the summer.

Enjoy the superb views east to the Little Orme and west to Conwy Mountain, Snowdonia and along the coast to Anglesey.

Continue to follow the waymarkers as you slowly descend, zigzagging down the steep hillside. After bearing right for some distance steadily descending, you eventually meet a flat grassy path at a waymarker, signed 'to Town'. Turn left onto this grassy path that contours around the hillside.

Continue on this open path until you reach the corner of an old stone wall, with housing visible ahead on left. Continue ahead, keeping the stone wall on your left but taking the lower path through the gorse that bears slightly away from the wall.

5 As you near the housing look for a waymarker post, signed 'to Town'. Turn right here onto a narrow stone-stepped path and follow this as it winds down the hillside.

Large numbers of butterflies are often seen along this sheltered path during the summer. Look for blue butterflies, mainly the common blue but the rare silver studded blue also breeds on the Great Orme.

At bottom of hill the natural path meets a tarmac path. To rejoin the **official route** turn right and follow tarmac path back to rejoin Marine Drive on the West Shore side. (If you are doing a circular walk, turn left here and follow this flat path, 'Invalid's Walk', back to Llandudno town.)

6 On the **official route** continue along the seafront at **West Shore**. Pass the **paddling pool** on the left and continue along the promenade.

The beach here is popular with kite-surfers, skimming across the water and twisting in the air, against the magnificent mountain backdrop.

View to Snowdonia from West Shore

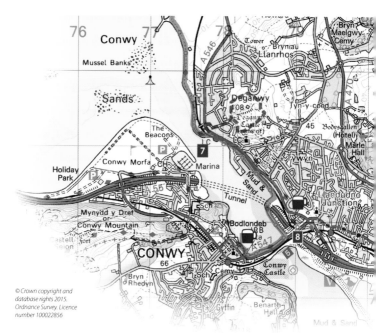

© Crown copyright and
database rights 2015.
Ordnance Survey. Licence
number 100022856

Llandudno was the favoured holiday destination for the Liddell family, whose daughter Alice was the inspiration for Alice in Wonderland, written by the Rev Dodgson under the pen name of Lewis Carroll. The family built a holiday home at Penmorfa on West Shore and it is thought that the Rev Dodgson, may have visted them there. The town is proud of its links with Alice. In 1933 Lloyd George unveiled a marble White Rabbit sculpture on West Shore. It has recently been restored and re-erected on Gloddaeth Street and there is now an Alice in Wonderland walking trail with digital augmented reality.

At the end of the promenade cross a car park, heading towards the Coast Path waymarker. Follow the narrow path, which is surfaced but often covered with sand, with the beach below to the right and dunes on the left, enjoying good views across 👁 **the Conwy Estuary**.

7 Emerge onto a tarmac path at **Deganwy**, walking along the small promenade with houses on the left. Continue to the railway crossing.

Detour: *To explore the Vardre or for facilities in Deganwy*
Cross the railway and continue along **Marine Crescent** to join the A546, **Station Road**. Carefully cross the busy road. Turn right for shops and refreshments but, to reach the Vardre, turn left and then first right onto

The remains of Henry III's castle on the Vardre

A hilltop stronghold

The Vardre was fiercely fought over for centuries

It is hard to imagine that the seaside village of Deganwy has a turbulent history, but The Vardre, the twin peaked hill overlooking Deganwy and the estuary, was a site of strategic military importance for over a thousand years. It was firecely fought over and changed hands many times. 6th century leader Maelgwyn Gywnedd held his court here. Norman knight, Robert of Rhuddlan, built a castle here in 1080 but it was regained by the Welsh and later destroyed in the reign of King John. The Welsh took control again in 1213 and rebuilt the castle but they destroyed it in 1240 to prevent the English making use of it. Henry III rebuilt it in stone, making it was one of his most powerful strongholds in Wales but, in 1263, after a long siege it was captured by Welsh Prince, Llywelyn ap Dafydd. Llywelyn systematically dismantled the castle so it could not easily be used for miltary purposes again. Henry's son Edward I chose to build a new castle at Conwy on the western bank of the river rather than trying to rebuild here and the castle on the Vardre was abandoned.

All that remains today are a few courses of stone from this once great castle.

More information: www.castlewales.com/deganwy.html and the website of Deganwy History Group has a downloadable walk: www.Deganwy History.co.uk

Beside the water: *Pretty terraced houses edge the shore at Deganwy*

York Road. Continue into **Gannock Park**, ignoring the turnings on the right and left (Gannock Park is circular). Partway up the hill, immediately after the entrance to **Plas Gwyn,** turn left along an enclosed footpath then go through a kissing gate onto open grassland. Turn left and follow a narrow natural path that contours round the hillside and slowly climbs, giving good views of the ruined castle on the hilltop to the right and across the estuary. Just beyond the first summit, turn right and walk across the dip between the small peaks. Bear right beside a panel on a stone plinth and follow the natural path back to the kissing gate. From here, retrace your steps back to the Coast Path.

In medieval times, Deganwy was the crossing point for the ferry across the Conwy but it was the opening of the railway line in 1858 that triggered the development of the gentile little resort we see today. Hotels opened near the station and a promenade was built linking the village with Llandudno's West Shore. Paddle steamers sailed from Deganwy on pleasure trips along the River Conwy to Trefriw until the outbreak of the Second World War. It was also an important port, exporting slate brought by rail from Blaenau Ffestiniog.

On the **official route**, turn right just before the railway crossing onto a narrow path and walk alongside the railway. At the entrance to **Deganwy Quay**, cross the access road and continue on a narrow path alongside railway.

Beyond Deganwy Quay there are good views across to Conwy, with the river crossings in the foreground, overlooked by the mighty castle. Looking at the three bridges that now span the river it is hard to imagine that until 1826, when Telford built the beautiful suspension bridge, a ferry was the only way to cross! George Stephenson's tubular railway bridge was completed in time for the opening of the railway in 1848 and the modern road bridge was built in 1958 when the suspension bridge was no longer suitable for the increasing amount of traffic.

Follow the path as it curves right away from railway, along the estuary, now walking on a more natural grey shingle path. Pass some sculptures on the left and continue to where the path meets a tarmac path just below the main road.

8 Turn right here and cross the **Conwy Bridge**. Turn right and walk down onto the quayside in **Conwy**, a perfect place to end this Day Section. To go into the town for shops, refreshments and accommodation, turn left under either of the stone arches in the old town walls that run along the waterfront.

The impressive view of Conwy Castle from Deganwy

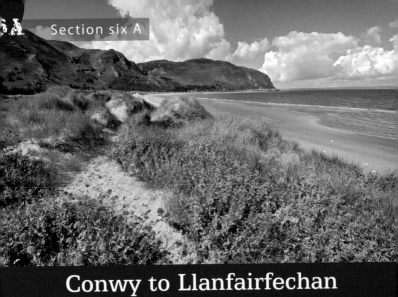

Conwy to Llanfairfechan
Coastal Route

Distance: *9 miles/ 14.5 kilometres* | **Start:** *Conwy riverside SH 783776*
Finish: *Llanfairfechan SH 679754* | **Maps:** *OS Landranger 115 Snowdon; and Explorer Outdoor Leisure 17 Snowdon*

Outline: An easy walk of two parts; a peaceful walk following the coast round Morfa Conwy and then alongside the A55 to Llanfairfechan

Allow time to explore historic Conwy, then from Conwy Quay the route follows a pretty path alongside the estuary to Conwy Marina, and continues along a sandy path round Morfa Conwy with great views across the estuary. The path then meets A55 at the first tunnel, and follows a path running parallel with the trunk road before descending to the coast again at Penmaenmawr. From here the path climbs and skirts the A55 before descending into Llanfairfechan.

Services: *All facilities in Conwy; pub and restaurant at Conwy Marina, beachside cafe at Penmaenmawr and refreshments, accommodation and shops in the village; B&Bs, shops and pubs in Llanfairfechan village and cafes on the promenade; railway stations at Conwy, Penmaenmawr and Llanfairfechan*

👁 **Don't miss:** Conwy Castle and town walls – well preserved Medieval castle and walls | **Morfa Conwy** – sandunes and wide views | **Penmaenmawr** – part Victorian resort and part granite quarrying village

▲ *Penmaenbach from Morfa Conwy*

Conwy

This little town is one of the most picturesque in Wales, one of Britain's best-preserved medieval towns. Set on the Conwy Estuary, it is dominated by the imposing castle and walls, with colourful fishing boats and sailing craft moored at the quayside or bobbing on the water below. Nowadays the atmosphere is relaxed and friendly, but the towers and high stone walls, are a reminder of its more turbulent past.

In 1186 Cistercian monks founded Aberconwy Abbey here (built on the site of the present church) on land granted to them by Welsh Prince, Llywelyn Fawr (the Great). King Edward I recognised the strategic importance of the site during his invasion of Wales and, in 1283, moved the Abbey up the river to Maenan so that he could build his formidable fortress and fortified town.

Medieval Conwy was a garrison town with English settlers living inside the walled town and the native Welsh forced to live outside. Resentments were strong and it was a site of conflict for centuries. In 1295 the town was besieged and Edward was trapped in his own castle. During Owain Glyndwr's revolt in 1401, the castle was captured without bloodshed when a Welsh sympathiser wedged open a door but the town was burned. By Tudor times the military importance of the castle had reduced and Welsh and English lived side by side.

In the 1800s the romantic ruins of the castle were drawing artists in search of the picturesque and this encouraged Victorian visitors, the beginnings of a new era for the town. In addition to Welsh and English, you may hear many other languages as the town now attracts visitors from around the world.

Conwy waterfront, dominated by the imposing castle

The route: **Conwy to Llanfairfechan** – Coastal Route

1 From **Conwy Quay**, walk along the waterfront, passing the Liverpool Arms and the smallest house in Wales on the left. Head to the arch of Postern Gate in the 👁 **Town Walls.**

> **Detour:** *Along the town walls (lots of steep steps and surface of wall-walk can be uneven!)*

At the end of the quay, go under the arch of Postern Gate then turn left uphill. At the road junction turn left. Go under the arch in the walls and immediately left up the steps onto the walls. After enjoying the views of the estuary from the Watchtower, turn left and along the wall-walk. Continue along the walls above the town until you reach the railway

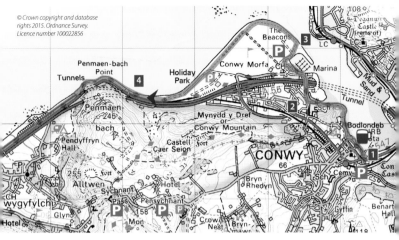

© Crown copyright and database rights 2015. Ordnance Survey. Licence number 100022856

where the walls have been breached. Descend steps here then turn left and immediate left again under an arch. Follow the path alongside a car park then turn left to go under a tunnel. At the end of the tunnel turn left up steps and continue under the arch ahead. Turn right and climb up steps in the tower to rejoin the wall-walk then follow to the car park beside the castle. Go down steps and cross the car park.

(👁 **Conwy Castle** entrance is on the right).

Turn right and walk along the pavement. At the busy road junction cross carefully and walk down paved path in front of the Knight's shop (small garden on the right). Go under an arch in the wall back onto the quayside. Turn left along the quayside to pick up the Coast Path once again.

Conwy's medieval town walls are some of the best preserved in Britain. They were built in the 1280s at the same time as the castle to give protection to the English settlers who were going to live in the new town. They remain almost fully intact today. There are three twin-towered gates and twenty one look-out towers at regular intervals which would have provided formidable defences. The wall-walk linking the towers was built to enable soldiers to keep lookout and swiftly move around the walls in case of attack.

A list of the 99 residents in 1295 indicated that the town was still exclusively English. By the 1300s a few Welsh names began to appear but tensions continued for many years and the Welsh were not allowed to become a sheriff or Royal Officer in the predominantly English town.

Estuary view: *Superb views across the estuary to Deganwy and the Vardre*

On the **official route**, go under the arch at Postern Gate then take the first lane on the right. Continue on a tarmac path alongside the estuary, passing the woodland of **Coed Bodlondeb** on the left and then school buildings. **2** Where path reaches road beside **Ysgol Aberconwy,** turn right following the blue and yellow Coast Path waymarkers, not the red and yellow ones to the left. Continue along road, crossing the bridge over the A55.

At a T junction turn left along **Ellis Way**. Take the first lane on right into **Telford Close** then follow the walkway between metal railings onto the marina. Turn left and walk along marina edge, with houses on the left. At the end of the marina turn right onto a road and, a few metres later turn left into **Beacon's Way launch site** and car park. Bear right, following waymarker, and walk through the car park to the coast at ☛ **Morfa Conwy**.

Morfa Conwy was used as a base for constructing sections of the Mulberry Harbour that was used in the Dee Day Landings in the Second World War. Code-named Mulberry, these floating harbours were constructed under great secrecy at a number of places along the coast. They were vital to the success of the Normandy landings and the remains of these harbours can still be seen along the French coast today.

They were designed by Welsh engineer Hugh Iorys Hughes of Bangor. He had proposed his idea to the War Office in 1941 and was commissioned by Winston Churchill to develop the prototype. It consisted of floating piers attached to massive steel pylons that rested on the sea bed, linked by floating roadways. At the peak of operations about 10 acres of Morfa Conwy were used. During this time up to 900 men lived on the site, which was covered with huts, hangars and shelters. By mid 1944, most of the work had been completed.

Mussels and Pearls

Mussels have been gathered from the Conwy Estuary for centuries, not only for food but also for the high quality pearls that were sometimes found inside them. In the 19th century Conwy pearls were sent to London jewellers and one may even have been used in the Crown Jewels. Pearls are no longer commonly found but the mussels continue to be a sought after delicacy today. In the summer months you can find out more at the Conwy Mussel Centre on the harbour.

Conwy Castle

Castles and Conquest

Designed to impress and intimidate

During the Middle Ages relationships between the English kings and the Welsh princes were tense. Llywelyn ap Gruffydd, had fought against Henry III in 1244, but made peace in 1267, when he was recognized as Prince of Wales. However in 1272, when Edward I succeeded his father, the situation changed. Edward was a seasoned military leader and determined to have a stronger control of Wales than his weak father.

In 1277 the relationship between Edward and Llywelyn reached breaking point after Llywelyn refused to pay homage to the king. Edward took decisive action, gathering a massive army in Chester and marching into Wales. His plans extended far beyond the immediate battles. To enable him to hold onto and strengthen his grip on the country Edward decided to build a string of impregnable castles along the Welsh

North-east tower, Flint Castle

coast. They were built to impress and intimidate but were also formidable military bases. Access by sea was essential, allowing for the castles to be supplied and reinforced if under siege from inland.

By the time Llywelyn was defeated in November 1277, work was well underway at Flint, the site of Edward's first castle, just one day's march from Chester. Rhuddlan was the second of his 'iron ring', built beside the River Clwyd, inland from Rhyl. Edward straightened and dredged the river for over 2 miles, providing a deep-water channel so ships could sail up the river and moor below the castle. This imposing castle became his early administrative base in North Wales. It was here that the Statute of Rhuddlan was signed in 1284, creating the medieval boroughs and English administrative system that was imposed across Wales.

Conwy Castle was Edward's third castle, begun in 1283, following the crushing of a final uprising by Llywelyn and his brother Dafydd. His centre of command in the later stages of that campaign was on the western bank of the River Conwy.

Wide views from Conwy Castle

This became the site of Conwy Castle and fortified town, built on a high rock facing the river. The outer walls and towers were built at speed in late 1283 and 1284 to create a defensible shell. The internal castle and town walls were completed by 1287.

Conwy is perhaps the most beautiful of Edward's castles. 18th century naturalist and travel writer, Thomas Pennant certainly thought so.

> "Conwy is one of the finest examples of late 13th century and early 14th century military architecture in Europe."
>
> UNESCO World Heritage site citation

"From the road are most august views of the vast expanse of the river, and the majestic towers of Conwy. Similar views and old fortified towns, I have seen frequent on the Rhine, but in magnificence far inferior to these, our British glory."

Thomas Pennant, *A Tour in Wales*

More information: For visit details for Conwy, Rhuddlan and Flint castles, refer to Cadw's website: http://cadw.gov.wales

Granite headland: *View to Penmaenbach from Morfa Conwy*

In the late 1980s this area was the site of major engineering works once more. In 1991 Queen opened the A55 submersed tube tunnel under the Conwy. It was built in a casting basin in the water at the site of what is now Conwy Marina and sections were floated into position in the river.

3 Turn left and walk along the grassy path alongside the estuary, with good views to Deganwy on the opposite bank. When you reach a fenced off area of sand dunes, keep to the right walking along the foreshore (still accessible at high tide). During the winter months it is possible to walk through the dunes but from March to June it is closed to the public to protect the rare belted beauty moth which breeds here. Please follow the signs.

This is the only known place in Wales where this unusual moth breeds. The female is wingless so cannot crawl far, climbing fence posts or stems of plants to lay eggs. The larvae feed on sand dune plants such as birds foot trefoil. Females and larvae are at risk of trampling so it is important to avoid the fenced off area.

Leave the foreshore at the end of the fence, bearing left to rejoin the grassy path. Continue walking along the coast with the golf course on the left and now with wide views to the Great Orme and also to Puffin Island

and Anglesey. Follow the path through a narrow strip of sand dunes, now with Conwy Mountain ahead.

Where the path meets an access road, turn right and follow the road into a car park. At the end of the car park continue ahead on a clear tarmac path with caravans on the left and fenced off dunes on the right. Follow this path to a bridge crossing the railway. Beyond the bridge turn right to join the cycleway alongside the A55, just before the **Penmaenbach Tunnel.**

A town of two halves

The little town of Penmaenmawr has two different faces. The eastern side was the seaside resort with Victorian boarding houses, villas and hotels. The western end served the granite quarries above the town. The quarrymen and their families, were housed in rows of terraced workers cottages and the granite setts were exported from a wharf built below the town. Look for the quarry clock on the hillside that ordered the lives of the workers.

4 Follow the cycle path round the outside of the tunnel and continue as the path moves slightly away from the A55, now walking between the road and railway.

Alternative route: *Along the beach from Penmaenbach*
Partway along a path on the right goes under the railway bridge onto the foreshore, giving an alternative path to Penmaenmawr at low tide.
NB It is essential that you check tide times.

On the **official route,** continue along the cycle path running parallel with the A55, crossing under a footbridge and passing a roundabout. Continue as it descends to ☂ **Penmaenmawr** promenade, (cafés and toilets). Beyond the **Sailing Club**, go under the bridge then right up steps. At top of the steps turn left along the pavement, cross the road by a small roundabout and take the tarmac path along the front, following the waymarkers.

Detour: *To visit Penmaenmawr village*
At the top of the steps, turn right and walk along pavement. At the junction with Bangor Road turn left and continue to the village centre.

Once one of the most fashionable seaside resorts along the North Wales Coast, Penmaenmawr was the favoured resort of Victorian Prime Minister William Ewart Gladstone who spent many summers there. He commented, "I do not know of a more healthy place; a more satisfactory climate is not to be found to my knowledge in this country." Others drawn by the unique attractions of the little town included George Bernard Shaw and Edward Elgar.

5 On the **official route**, take the left-hand tarmac path, going under the A55 bridge. Walk uphill and left following signs, zig-

© Crown copyright and database rights 2015.
Ordnance Survey. Licence number 100022856

Coast and mountain: *The beach at Llanfairfechan with Penmaenbach behind*

zagging underneath the A55. Cross an access lane to cottages and go up a narrow walkway and steps to join a minor road. Cross the road and turn right, following clear signs for the cycle path and pedestrian walkway above the westbound A55 tunnel.

Follow this walkway, which runs above the eastern carriageway of A55, eventually crossing a footbridge to join a minor road on the left-hand side of the dual carriageway. Take the next right onto a small private road. Walk down the road, passing a barrier and continuing downhill to a T junction, with the A55 roundabout to the right. Turn left and walk along the pavement of **Penmaenmawr Road** into Llanfairfechan for shops and facilities.

Alternative route: *via promenade (does not pass shops)*
After a few metres cross the road and take the first right onto **Shore Street East**. Follow this narrow road downhill, going through a narrow tunnel to emerge at the coast. Turn left and walk along the promenade to the Beach Pavilion and car park at Llanfairfechan.

6 For the **official route**, continue on Penmaenmawr Road to traffic lights at the cross roads. Turn right down Station Road and follow this road to the coast, passing under the A55 bridge and then railway bridge (turn left here for railway station). This Day Section ends on the promenade by the Beach Pavilion café.

Menai Bridge

The road to Ireland

Feats of engineering were needed to build a road and railway along the North Wales coast

The rugged coast, with its treacherous tides, high cliffs, and wide estuaries at Conwy and the Menai Straits, presented challenges for travellers. Ferry was the only way to cross the estuaries but the currents were notorious and accidents were common. The precipitous headlands of Penmaenbach and Penmaenmawr presented further difficulties. At low tide the traveller could cross the sands to Llanfairfechan but, at high tide, the upland route using the Sychnant Pass and a difficult traverse above Penmaenmawr, was the only option.

The first mail service from London to Holyhead via Chester, used post boys on horses but, when the Mail Coaches were introduced, the route problems became more acute.

Telford's suspension bridge at Conwy

When the Act of Union was passed in 1800, traffic increased further, with Irish MPs travelling to and fro and increased mail between London and Ireland. On Christmas Day 1806, the Conwy ferry capsized with the loss of 13 lives. In 1807, the Bangor ferry crossing the Menai Strait capsized, drowning 14 people. It became clear that something had to be done.

In 1811, renowned engineer, Thomas Telford, was commissioned to survey the road from Shrewsbury to Holyhead to find an alternative route through North Wales. In 1815, he began work on the new A5 through Llangollen, Betws-y-Coed and Bangor, then spanning the Menai Straits with the magnificent Menai Suspension Bridge. His commission was extended to upgrade the Chester to Bangor coastal route. He created narrow roads around the headlands at Penmaenmawr and Penmaenbach (now used by pedestrians and cyclists) and crossed the River Conwy with a second suspension bridge, designing its towers to blend with the castle. The whole project was completed by 1826, enabling much swifter, safer travel to Holyhead.

Just twenty years later the railway

Royal Mail Coach

was built along the coast. It reduced the journey from London to Holyhead from over 24 hours to 9 hours 30mins. Another great engineer, Robert Stephenson, masterminded the work, building tubular railway bridges to cross the estuaries, and tunnels through the headlands.

The arrival of the motor car put new pressures on the coast road. In the 1980s, in response to severe summer traffic jams caused by the increased traffic, the 'Road to Ireland' was upgraded once more, creating the A55 dual carriageway. Cutting edge engineering was used once again to construct a tunnel under the Conwy Estuary and additional long tunnels through the headlands.

> *"The Menai Suspension Bridge was the longest in the world when it was built, 597 feet of deck held up by sixteen huge chains."*

More information: Telford Centre, Menai Bridge 01248 715046/ www.menaibridges.co.uk

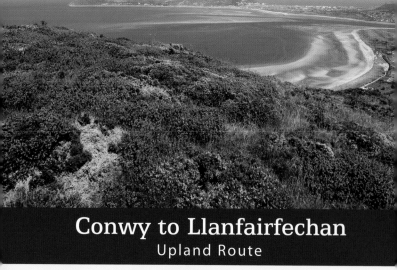

Conwy to Llanfairfechan
Upland Route

Distance: *11 miles/ 18 kilometres* | **Start:** *Conwy riverside SH 783776*
Finish: *Llanfairfechan SH 679754* | **Maps:** *OS Landranger 115 Snowdon; and
Explorer Outdoor Leisure 17 Snowdon*

Outline: **A** superb but more demanding upland walk along the heathery ridge of Conwy Mountain, then rounding Foel Lus and crossing open
moorland before descending to Llanfairfechan.

From the quayside at Conwy, follow a pleasant path alongside the estuary,
then a short section on quiet lanes until climbing through woodland onto
the open ridge of Conwy Mountain. With panoramic views to the coast and
Snowdonia, the route follows natural paths across the heather covered ridge,
before descending to the Sychnant Pass. It then follows a quiet lane through
Capelulo before climbing again onto Foel Lus, joining the Victorian Jubilee
Walk, then crossing wild moorland dotted with standing stones before descending slowly through pasture and woodland to Llanfairfechan.

Services: *All facilities in Conwy; B&Bs, shops, cafes, pubs and toilets in Llanfairfechan;
pub and hotels at Capelulo, railway stations at Conwy and Llanfairfechan*

👁 **Don't miss:** Conwy Mountain – beautiful heathery ridge with magnifi-
cent views | **Druids' circle and standing stones** – ancient sites of ritual on the
open moorland | **Llanfairfechan seafront** – Pretty Victorian pavilion and beach

▲   *View to the Great Orme from Conwy Mountain*

Conwy

Although the castle dominates the town visually, it is the quay that has been its lifeblood. Fishing and trade has always played a big part in the life of the town and the quay has been at the hub. The wooden quay was rebuilt in stone in 1831 and has withstood the battering of the tides ever since The quayside and side streets in the town are lined with small fishermen's cottages. None are smaller than the tiny red cottage beside the Liverpool Arms, the smallest house in Britain, only 72" wide and 122" high but reputedly once occupied by a 6'3" fisherman! The Liverpool Arms was the favoured haunt of the Conwy mariners and is still thriving today.

Crossfield's boatyard was established in the late 1900s, building wooden fishing boats. In 2009, traditional boat building returned to the quayside, with an ongoing project to restore one of the boats built at Crossfield's. The Helen II which is a 'Nobby prawner', a traditional wooden sailing boat that was used by fishermen along the North Wales coast and Liverpool Bay at the end of the 19th century.

Understandably the town is renowned for its fish and chips, made using freshly caught fish. They are best enjoyed sitting at the harbour watching the boats on a summer's evening but look out for the greedy seagulls!

Fishing boats and leisure craft mix at Conwy Quay

The route: **Conwy to Llanfairfechan** – Upland Route

1 From **Conwy Quayside**, walk along the quay, passing the **Liverpool Arms** on the left and continue under the arch in the **Town Walls** and follow the road up the hill. Take the first lane on the right (marked with both green North Wales Path and blue Wales Coast Path waymarkers).

The quay at Conwy has been in use for centuries, originally built to provide mooring for Edward I's ships in the 13th century but later serving the thriving river port. Shipwrights built sloops and schooners here using oak that was floated down the river from Gwydir Forest. Copper from the Great Orme mines was transported to Swansea for smelting and South Wales coal brought back; grain was transported to Ireland and Liverpool. Fishermen still land their catches at the quay, both deep sea fish like plaice and cod but also the famous Conwy mussels. Leisure craft mingle with the fishing boats now and the estuary is always full of activity.

Follow the tarmac path alongside the estuary, with the woodland of **Coed Bodlondeb** on the left, then passing school buildings.

2 Where the path reaches road beside **Ysgol AberConwy**, turn left, now following red and yellow Coast Path markers, indicating the official upland route. These are the waymarkers you will be following throughout this walk. (Some of the route is shared with the North Wales Path so you will see many of the green waymarkers too.)

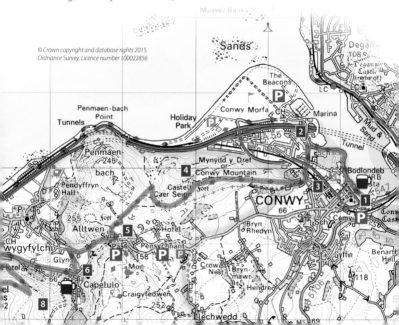

© *Crown copyright and database rights 2015.*
Ordnance Survey. Licence number 100022856

Encircling walls: *Mill Gate in Conwy's town walls gave access to the royal watermill*

Follow the road to a T junction with the main road. Cross the main road carefully and follow a drive ahead, then cross the railway via the footbridge. Follow the clear path between two stone walls to emerge onto a tarmac lane. Ignore the entrance to **Beechwood Court** on right and continue to another junction. Turn right and continue uphill along the lane.

3 Just beyond housing where the lane forks, take the right-hand fork then follow the drive uphill. Just past a cottage take the natural path up steps to cross the stile visible ahead. Follow the natural path uphill through scrub woodland and onto the open hillside. Where the path splits take the lower fork, walking ahead on the lower path, signed North Wales Path.

Detour: *Short detour for superb views*

Turn right and walk over a small summit to enjoy the views across the estuary to the Great Orme before retracing your sets to rejoin the official route.

Continue on same path along the left-hand side of 👁 **Conwy Mountain**, enjoying the views of the Sychnant Pass and the Snowdonian mountains to the left. Ignore paths left and right before the large slabs on the right. Continue ahead where a path joins from the right, following the Coast Path waymarker. Just before a large boulder on the left, look for a panel on the right describing the remains of the hillfort.

Along the ridge: *Refreshing walking on Conwy Mountain, with good views of the Great Orme*

Caer Seion Iron Age hillfort was built over 2000 years ago, positioned in an ideal defensive location with commanding views from all sides. Deep ditches and 3metre high stone ramparts encircled the settlement which consisted of a number of roundhouses. The Iron Age people were farmers and traders. Remains of stone spinning weights have been found here, which suggests they kept sheep, and they may have traded metal implements by sea. They were also prepared for attack as over 400 sling shots were found inside the main entrance. It would have been a daunting place to attack. Imagine struggling up the steep hilllside carrying weapons and under fire!

4 Beyond the boulder, bear right at path fork, following the Coast Path way-markers along a narrow, meandering path through the heather and gorse, ignoring paths off to the left as you gradually climb. When the path joins a wider path turn left, now walking with the sea visible on the right. Pause to enjoy the magnificent views to the Great Orme on the right.

The small buildings on the hillsides are winding sheds for the old millstone quarries, built to house the winding drums that pulled the trucks up and down the hillsides, taking the quarried rock down to the port or railway at Conwy .

Where the path begins to descend, take a path left, signed Wales Coast Path, now walking inland again (If you want to savour the coastal views a little longer, detour by continuing to the hilltop ahead.)

Ignore a minor path fork, bearing right on the broader path. At a major path crossroads, continue ahead, following the waymarked path. Continue on this path as it descends. At the bottom of the hill, go through a gateway and cross a stream on stepping stones.

Carneddau ponies

Look out for the wild Carneddau ponies who roam the moorland throughout the year. Their ancestors could have been killed when Henry VIII, in an attempt to breed taller, stronger horses, decreed that all ponies below a certain height should be killed. He ordered an annual round up of all feral ponies but the wild mountainous terrain of the Carneddau enabled some ponies to evade capture and the breed is thought to have developed from these hardy animals.

Just beyond the stream, cross a wide farm track, and continue ahead up the grassy path opposite (signed North Wales Path). Where the path joins a track, turn right (Wales Coast Path waymarker) and follow this path downhill towards the **Sychnant Pass car park**.

5 Partway down this path, look for a low wooden waymarker post and, by the post, take a small path right down steps and follow this narrow path downhill. At a junction with a path leading from the car park, turn right and walk down the valley, continuing as path becomes a track and passes houses on both sides. Where the path meets a road turn right. Just after crossing a bridge, turn left along drive to **Y Glyn**, now walking with stream on left. Pass Y Glyn on the right and continue on path ahead to reach the road at **Capelulo**.

6 Turn right along road opposite the Austrian Restaurant, with the **Fairy Glen pub** and hotel to the left. Continue alongside the road for 1 mile/1.5 kilometres.

7 Immediately after passing **Treforris Road** on the right, take waymarked path on the left. Follow this grassy path behind housing. Go through a kissing gate, passing an old chapel on the left, following clear path alongside a wall, with housing on left and the open mountain to the right, gradually climbing.

Ignore a right-hand fork and continue along the wall. Look for a low way-marker post and turn right here, walking uphill to reach a grassy path (the bench to the left along that path is a useful marker but do not turn in that direction). Cross the path and continue ahead now climbing steeply up the bank, heading in the direction of a small stone building ahead.

When you reach a wider path just below the building, turn left and follow this clear path round the hillside, still climbing but less steeply now. Continue to the next path junction and turn left, following waymarker, still climbing.

Purple heather carpets Conwy Mountain in August

Open moorland: *The rounded tops of the Carneddau ahead*

---

8 At the top of this path by a finger post, turn right, but you may wish to have a well-earned rest on the bench first, enjoying the magnificent views of Conwy Mountain. Follow the clear path as it contours around the hillside of **Foel Lus** with magnificent views out to sea and of the quarrying above Penmaenmawr. At the end of the path pass between two tall stone pillars that were built to mark the opening of the Jubilee Path.

The Jubilee Path you have been walking on was built to enable Victorian visitors to enjoy the panoramic views and named to commemorate Queen Victoria's Golden Jubilee in 1887.

The hard granite from the mountainside above Penmaenmawr has been quarried since 1830 and quarrying still continues today. Granite was in demand across Europe, mainly as setts for road building and stone from Penmaenmawr was exported from the wharf at the western end of the village. The mountainside has been so heavily quarried that its height has reduced from over 1500' to 1000'.

9 Just beyond the pillars where the path meets a narrow road, keep left on the higher path, slowly climbing. Follow this clear path, passing a bench and an attractive stone waymarker. There are several paths here but continue ahead and then take the right-hand fork at a 'no entry' sign. Keep on this clear track. Go through a metal kissing gate and continue along the track.

Endless views: *The magnificent views along the coast are a wonderful feature of this walk*

At a finger post where North Wales Path is signed left, continue ahead along the track. Go through another gateway and continue, passing a white cottage on the right.

The large round boulder in the field to the left is an erratic, moved and shaped by a glacier. Four thousand years ago it may have been stood up and used as a marker post by prehistoric people.

Just beyond house look for a waymarker post with several discs, including the Coast Path. Turn right here and walk uphill on a narrower path. Go through the metal kissing gate ahead onto open ground.

Continue uphill for a few metres then bear left at waymarker, following the clear path. Continue on this path across the open moorland, slowly climbing.

Detour: *Druids' Circle standing stones*
Partway along the path you can detour left on a grassy path to visit the 👁 **Druids' Circle** which is clearly visible on the skyline.

10 Continue along the moorland path, soon walking with a stone wall on the right. Where this grassy path joins a more major track, continue in the same direction, walking parallel with the coast. At the corner of the stone

wall, bear right at path fork (leaving the North Wales Path), following the clearly waymarked wide grassy path across the moorland.

Pass an old stone sheepfold on left. Keep ahead where a wider path bears right, walking with a stone wall on the left and good views to Anglesey and the Menai Strait. Go through a wooden kissing gate then turn left, following a clear track downhill.

The Druids' Circle

Meini Hirion (the long stones) is the largest of the numerous ceremonial circles, standing stones, and burial mounds that were built on the mountainside by prehistoric peoples. It is thought to have been built in the Bronze Age, about 3400 years ago and would have been an important spiritual site. Cremated bones have been found in a burial chamber within the circle. It became known as the 'Druids' Circle' in Victorian times, although it was built long before the time of the druids!

11 Where the track turns sharply left, turn right off the track by a fingerpost. Walk alongside the wall on the left, walking downhill on a grassy path towards the coast. Go through a kissing gate and continue downhill through the field. Go through a gap in a stone wall and continue ahead, ignoring path signed right, descending on the meandering grassy path through gorse, with crags to the right. At a path junction bear left by a waymarker post and walk downhill. Go through a metal kissing gate and follow the sunken path down to farm buildings.

12 At a path junction in front of houses and the farmyard, turn sharp right then walk past the old farm outbuildings, and go through a gateway into a large field. Continue straight ahead, walking down the field. Look for a waymarker near the bottom of field and turn half-right here. Walk downhill for a few metres and then bear right following an old stone wall and walking towards a gateway ahead.

Go through a kissing gate and down steps. Continue ahead through small wooden gates still descending. At the bottom of the steps, pass a house on the left and go through another metal gate. Follow the path between low stone walls and then through a metal kissing gate into **Tyddyn Drycin**, a woodland nature reserve.

Turn left at a path T junction, following the path downhill through the woodland. Continue descending,

© Crown copyright and database
rights 2015. Ordnance Survey.
Licence number 100022856

Quarry terraces: *The mountainside above Penmaenmawr has been heavily quarried*

passing housing on the left. Turn left downhill at the next, then go through another kissing gate, leaving **Tyddyn Drycin**. Continue downhill, now with houses on the right.

13 Just past a cottage, take a path on the left up steps to a road. Cross the road and continue on the path ahead. At the end of the path, go through a small gate onto a road. Turn left and walk uphill along the road, following it round to the right. At the end of the road, by **Hafod-y-coed**, go through the gate ahead and continue along a private track through **Penmaen Park**.

At end of the park go through a metal gate onto a road and continue ahead along the road, soon with housing on both sides. Pass the **Church Institute** on the right and then turn right at the road junction.

The whitewashed Institute is one of several Arts and Crafts movement buildings in this part of Llanfairechan, designed by architect Herbert North at the turn of the twentieth century.

At the road junction opposite the Co-op, turn right and follow the road to traffic lights in the centre of the village. Cross the road at the lights and continue ahead down **Station Road**. Follow this to the coast, passing under the A55 bridge and then railway bridge (turn left here for railway station). This Day Section ends on 🐾 **Llanfairfechan promenade** by the Beach Pavilion café.

Rescue boats around the 'Thetis'

Shipwrecks and gales

Many ships and lives have been lost in these treacherous waters

Shipping was a key part of the economy of the North Wales coast but sailing these waters was a risky business and they have claimed many lives. An RNLI Wreck Chart from July 1897 to June 1898 shows a greater concentration of wrecks along the Dee Estuary, the Great Orme and the Menai Strait than anywhere else in Wales. The ever-changing sand bars in the Dee Estuary, strong currents, cliffs and submerged rocks around the Great Orme and Anglesey, coupled with severe storms, make navigation extremely hazardous.

The Rothesay Castle, one of the paddle steamers used for pleasure trips from Liverpool along the North Wales Coast, was wrecked on Lavan Sands on 18th August 1931. The captain and mate were drunk and, when the weather deteriorated, missed the

Stormy skies over Talacre lighthouse

opportunity to land the ship safely at Llandudno. The ship was in poor condition; the pumps didn't work, it had no lantern to summon help and only one lifeboat, which had a hole in bottom and no oars! Of the 150 on board only 23 survived. The disaster led to the building of Penmon lighthouse on Puffin Island.

The storm of October 1859 not only wrecked the Royal Charter off Anglesey, with the cost of 400 lives, but also destroyed a newly built pier at Llandudno, scattering its broken timbers on the beach and ruining the town's hopes of developing as a port to challenge Holyhead for the Irish trade.

A great storm that raged for two days in November 1890 hit the little port of Connah's Quay hard. The journal of the local minister records 'almost every door in Connah's Quay had a wreath upon it, forty vessels having left the Roads that fateful morning ….'

In 1939 the Royal Navy suffered its worst peacetime submarine disaster when the submarine HMS Thetis sank 12 miles off the Great Orme. She had been built at Cammell Laird's shipyard in Birkenhead and was on sea trials, carrying 103 men, twice

Penmon lighthouse

the number she was designed for, with engineers from Cammell Laird and observers as well as the crew. A catalogue of problems resulted in sea water flooding in and the submarine nose-dived and couldn't resurface. Oxygen was in short supply due to the large numbers on board but help was slow to come. Four men escaped through a hatch but 99 suffocated inside the submarine.

The seas remain challenging today. In 2012, the severe winter storm grounded a cargo boat loaded with limestone off Colwyn Bay. During the winter storms the following year, the sea breached the sea wall in several places, causing widespread damage and closing large stretches of the Coast Path.

More information: http://www.llandudno.com/wrecks.html

> *"White foam, like a mist, covered the bay as a hurricane force wind drove the huge breakers ashore."*
>
> Contemporary account of the 1859 storm at Llandudno

Llanfairfechan to Bangor

Distance: *9½ miles/ 15.5 kilometres* | **Start:** *Llanfairfechan SH 679754*
Finish: *Bangor Pier SH 585732* | **Maps:** *OS Landranger 115 Snowdon; and Explorer Outdoor Leisure 17 Snowdon*

Outline: An easy walk hugging the coast with views across the Menai Strait, then following quiet lanes and an old railway path into Bangor.

From Llanfairfechan promenade the route goes through the traditional park and then onto more open coast and saltmarsh. This central section is peaceful and picturesque, walking on natural paths and foreshore alongside coastal nature reserves. It is wonderful for birdwatching and there are good views across to Puffin Island, Anglesey and Penryhn Castle. The final section turns inland at Aber Ogwen, on lanes through Llandygai then following the disused railway line path to Porth Penrhyn, and onto Bangor, ending by the pier.

Services: *Shops, hotels, B&Bs and pubs in Llanfairfechan village and cafes on the promenade. Bangor is a bustling university city with lots of accommodation, supermarkets, shops, banks, post office, pubs, restaurants, cafés and takeaways. Cathedral, museum and pier. Railway stations at Llanfairfechan and Bangor.*

Don't miss: Coastal nature reserves – wonderful for birdwatching | **Penrhyn Castle** – a Victorian gothic castle | **Bangor Pier** – a classic Edwardian seaside pier

▲ *View from the saltmarsh at Morfa Aber*

Llanfairfechan

The little town of Llanfairechan still has a gentile feel with many Victorian and Edwardian buildings. The shops line the main road running down to the coast and the attractive promenade is the focal point for the beach.

It was little more than a hamlet until the nineteenth century with only occasional travellers passing through on the hazardous journey to Holyhead and Ireland, either coming along the shore between the tides or attempting dangerous climb over the mountain.

The town's development began in the middle of the 19th century, following the upgrading of the coast road by Thomas Telford. The opening of the railway in 1845 improved access further although, at first, the nearest stop was neighbouring Abergwyngregyn. The growing town attracted some prominent businessmen and there was pressure to build the station at Llanfairfechan to enable easier travel to London. The town developed rapidly after this, becoming a popular holiday resort with its promenade, guest houses, hotels and sea-front pavilion (now a café).

Llanfairfechan beach

The route: **Llanfairfechan to Bangor**

1 From the **Beach Pavilion Café** at **Llanfairfechan** turn left along the promenade. Go through a kissing gate into the park then follow the clear path along the sea front, passing the boating lake.

Beyond the park go through another kissing gate alongside a small area of woodland on the left and continue along the clear path. You are now passing through ❧ **Glan y Môr Elias Nature Reserve**. Follow the path as it bends left, now walking inland with a fence on the left and saltmarsh to the right.

Continue ahead at a path junction, ignoring wide grassy path right, passing a house on the left and crossing a stream feeding into the estuary. At the waymarker in front of a row of upright slate fence posts, turn right and walk back out to the coast along a grassy natural path. Bear left along the coast.

The mix of sand, mudflats and saltmarsh of Lavan Sands provide a superb habitat for wildlife and there are a series of coastal nature reserves along this section to conserve the habitats. The invertebrates in the rich estuarine mud provide plentiful food for fish and birds alike. Thousands of birds overwinter on the estuary before flying to their arctic breeding grounds and many others pass through on migration.

© Crown copyright and database rights 2015.
Ordnance Survey. Licence number 100022856

Lagoons and inlets: *The flat saltmarsh is a rich feeding ground for both sheep and birdlife*

2 Do not go through wooden gate into 👁 **Morfa Madryn Nature Reserve**, but instead continue along the coast with the slate fence of the nature reserve on the left.

This section is superb for bird watching with lagoons and saltmarsh on the left and mudflats on the right. The saltmarsh and wet meadows provide feeding, breeding and roosting areas for birds such as lapwings and redshank. Listen too for skylarks, singing high in the sky.

Follow the grassy path along the coast with the fence on the left and, where this path ends, continue walking on shingle along the top of the beach. Continue ahead hugging the coast, then go through a kissing gate onto an enclosed path between fields and the coast. Eventually go through a gate on the right to return to the coast and turn left, walking along a grassy path above the shore.

Go across a small footbridge over the river and continue ahead through another gate onto boardwalk. Ignore a gate into woodland ahead, and follow the path right through a smaller gate. Continue walking on a stone path alongside the coast with good views ahead to 👁 **Penrhyn Castle.**

Pass a bird hide on the right and follow the path as it bears left and slightly inland. Go through a gap by a wooden gate, then past a metal barrier beside the entrance to **Morfa Aber car park.**

Detour: *Aber Falls*

Two miles inland are the magnificent Aber Falls that plunge over 120'
from the Carneddau mountains to the valley below. They are well worth
a trip but you would need to allow a half day to make the most of them.
(Detailed directions are not given here, refer to OS Explorer OL17.)

3 Turn left along the road and right soon after onto an access track. Continue
along the track, passing a house on the left. Where the track ends, descend
to the foreshore and continue ahead, carefully picking your way over large
boulders and stone slabs at first (still present at time of writing) but it levels
out eventually. There are good views of 👁 **Penrhyn Castle** along this stretch.

*From a distance Penrhyn looks like another of the imposing medieval coastal
castles, strategically positioned to control the Menai Strait. However it is a fantasy
castle built in the nineteenth century in neo-norman style for George Dawkins-
Pennant on the proceeds from the family sugar plantations in Jamaica and their
local slate quarries. It is now owned by the National Trust. The gothic castle was
greatly admired and visited by the rich and influential. Famous visitors included
Queen Victoria who slept in a specially made one ton slate bed!*

Continue walking along the grassy bank above the beach, with a fence
on the left. Go through a wooden kissing gate then turn right to follow
the enclosed grassy path alongside fields, running parallel with the coast.
Continue on this clear path, slightly climbing, with good views across the
Menai Strait. Go through a wooden gate still following the clear path, now
with a woodland strip on the right.

Go through a kissing gate on the right back onto the foreshore. Go left
down steps, now walking above pebbly foreshore, and follow the path into
Aber Ogwen car park.

Imposing grandeur: *There are good views of Victorian gothic Penrhyn Castle*

On the headland you may be able to pick out a little jetty. This is the site of the sea baths that the Lord Penrhyn had built to give private bathing for the family.

4 Turn left and walk down the quiet road, passing the **Spinnies Nature Reserve** on the right. Continue along the road crossing over the railway. At a T junction turn right and walk along the pavement on the right-hand side. After 100 metres cross the road and turn left down a smaller road, following signs for **Talybont** and **Rachub.**

5 Just before the church, where a road joins from the left, turn right through a small metal gate, onto a narrow path alongside the church. Follow the enclosed path then go through a kissing gate into a field. Follow the left-hand field edge to the field corner, then go left through a metal kissing gate.

Walk down the right-hand fenceline alongside the railway. Go through a kissing gate and walk to the road. Turn right along road, walking under the railway bridge and continue to the road junction.

Turn left at the road junction, with the side entrance to the Penrhyn Estate opposite, then carefully cross the busy road opposite the bus stop, and continue in the same direction. Cross over the **Afon Ogwen** and just beyond the bridge as you are nearing the village of Llandegai, cross the road and take the path on the left, signed **Tre Felin**, now walking along the access road to **Celtest.**

Rainbow's end: *There's a real sense of space where the saltmarsh edges the Menai Straits*

Llandegai village was developed by the owner of Penrhyn Castle as a 'model village' to house his estate workers. He did not allow the building of a 'corrupting ale-house'!

Just before entrance to **Celtest**, turn right along little lane, past Trefelin cottages on left and with the railway bridge ahead. Beyond the cottages go under the railway bridge then turn right by a fingerpost, walking up a path to a white cottage. Turn right in front of the cottage and follow the drive.

Where the drive bears left past a machinery depot, keep going ahead along a narrow path. Climb up steps at end of the path onto a road. Cross this road and then turn left along a second road. Walk along the pavement to the end of the road where it meets the main **A5.** Turn left at the road junction and then carefully cross the main road just before the roundabout.

6 Turn left and immediate right beside a road with a barrier across the entrance (at time of writing). Walk along the pavement, continuing downhill to a roundabout at the end of the road. Turn right onto a clear wide path and follow this to a minor road, passing wetland and scrub on the right.

Turn left and walk along the road. Where the road descends to a ford,

turn sharply left just before the footbridge through a black metal gate, then left again onto the tarmac cycleway.

You are now walking along the former track of the railway line that was built to transport slates from Lord Penrhyn's quarry at Bethesda to Porth Penrhyn for export. At first trucks were pulled along a tramway by horses but, from 1878, a new steam railway opened. The railway operated until 1962.

7 Follow this clear path for about 1¼ miles/2 kilometres towards Bangor,

Wetland breeding ground

Lapwings, easily recognised by their irridescent green tinged plumage and distinctive crest, are just one of the many species that of the nest on the saltmarsh at Morfa Madryn. You may hear their piercing 'peewit' call. Their numbers in England and Wales have declined by 80% since 1987, mainly due to changes in farming, so undisturbed habitats such as this are very important for their survival.

passing under the railway bridge and later under a road bridge. Eventually cross two footbridges over the river and continue ahead to the coast. Go under a small bridge and then the cycle path emerges at the estuary at **Porth Penrhyn**.

At the end of the nineteenth century Bethesda Quarry was the largest quarry in the world and trade from Porth Penrhyn would have been brisk. The scene would have looked very different with tonnes of slates being loaded onto schooners for export across the world. It is much more peaceful nowadays but is still a working port and boatyard, used by fishing and leisure boats. The slate slabs that edge the jetties remind of its former history.

Turn left onto the access road walking away from the port. At the junction with the main road, turn right along pavement and follow the road downhill towards **Bangor** town centre.

8 Just beyond a park, turn right through a car park and onto a small section of promenade. At the end of the promenade, go through a gap beside a barrier and turn right along a minor road with new housing on the left and the the estuary to the right. (Additional housing was being built at the time of writing so directions may slightly change.) Continue along the lane, following signs for **Cycle Route 5** and passing a small stoney bay on the right. At a T junction, turn right along **Garth Road** and continue to 👁 **Bangor Pier.** This is the end of your walk but be sure to walk out onto the pier to enjoy the wonderful views across the Menai Strait and to enjoy its Edwardian charms.

Pretty Bangor Pier was opened in 1896 by Lord Penryhn. Paddle steamers from the Isle of Man, Liverpool and Blackpool moored at the pier bringing passengers to the thriving seaside resort. It was renovated in 1988 and the twin onion domes, ornate shelters and pier end tea room, still remind of its Edwardian hey-day.

To continue into **Bangor** itself walk back along Garth Road to the junction with the main road. Turn right here and follow the road uphill to the town and railway station.

Bangor Pier where this section of the path finishes

Welsh coastal place names

Welsh place names are as much a part of Wales's cultural distinctiveness as its mountains, sheep or rugged coast. To the English visitor, they may appear strangely foreign, confusing or simply unpronounceable. And yet, once carefully unravelled, they can tell us all sorts of fascinating things about a place — its landscape, character and history. Even these few common place name elements should help bring the Wales Coast Path alive.

Aber	river mouth, estuary	*Ab-er*
Afon	river	*Av-on*
Bad	ferry, boat	*Bad*
Bae	bay	*Bai*
Cae	field, enclosure	*Kai*
Carreg	stone, rock	*Kar-egg*
Cawl	sea kale	*Kowl*
Cei	quay	*Kay*
Cilfach	cove, creek	*Kil-vakh*
Clegyr	rock, cliff	*Kleg-ir*
Culfor	strait	*Kil-vor*
Din/dinas	citadel; hillfort; fortified hill	*Deen/Deen-as*
Dwr/dwfr	water	*Doer/Doo-vr*
Dyffryn	valley; bottom	*Duff-ryn*
Eglwys	church	*Eg-looees*

Looking to the Great Orme from Morfa Conwy

Ffynnon	well; spring; fountain; source	*Fun-on*
Goleudy	lighthouse	*Gol-ay-dee*
Glan	shore	*Glan*
Gwymon	seaweed	*Gwi-mon*
Harbwr	harbour	*Harboor*
Heli	salt water, brine	*Hel-lee*
Llech	flat stone, flagstone, slate	*Th-lekh*
Maen	stone; standing stone	*Mine*
Mor	sea, ocean	*More*
Morfa	sea marsh, salt marsh	*Mor-va*
Moryd	estuary, channel	*Mor-rid*
Ogof	cave	*Og-ov*
Parrog	flat land by the sea	*Par-rog*
Penrhyn	headland	*Pen-rin*
Pigyn	point	*Pig-in*
Pont/bont	bridge, arch	*Pont/Bont*
Porth	harbour	*Porth*
Pwll	pool, pit	*Pooth*
Tafol	dock	*Tav-ol*
Ton/don	wave	*Ton/Don*
Traeth	beach	*Treye-th*
Trwyn	nose; point; cape	*Troo-een*
Tywyn	sandy shore sand dunes	*Tow-in*
Ynys	island	*Un-iss*

"*Wales, where the past still lives. Where every place has its tradition, every name its poetry ...*"

Matthew Arnold, *On the Study of Celtic Literature*, 1866

Visitor Information

Wales Coast Path

Comprehensive information about all sections of the Wales Coast Path can be found on the official website at **www.walescoastpath.gov.uk** and **www.walescoastpath.co.uk**

'Visit Wales'

The Visit Wales website covers everything from accommodation to attractions. For information on the area covered by this book, see: **www.visitwales. com/explore/north-wales/snowdonia-mountains-coast/**

North Wales Coast

For local information, from what to do and local history to eating out or finding accommodation, **www.visitflintshire.com; www.rhyl.com; www.rhyl-prestatyn.co.uk; www.visitllandudno.org.uk; www.visitconwytown. co.uk; www.llanfairfechan.org.uk; www.penmaenmawr.com**

Tourist Information Centres

The main TICs provide free information on everything from accommodation and travel to what's on and walking advice.

Rhyl: 01745 355068 Rhyl Childrens Village, West Parade, LL18 1HZ crhyl.tic@denbighshire.gov.uk

Llandudno: 01492 577577   Mostyn Street, LL30 2RP
Conwy: 01492 577566   Rose Hill Street, LL32 8LD

Where to stay

For most sections, there's lots of accommodation close to the Wales Coast Path, from campsites and B&Bs to holiday cottages and hotels (NB more sparse between Connah's Quay and Talacre). Tourist Information Centre staff will know what's available locally and can even book for you. Alternatively, book online. Find camp sites at **www.ukcampsite.co.uk**

Luggage Carrying Service

Cheap, door-to-door luggage transfer between overnight stops. 'Luggage Transfer' 01437 723 030 | **www.luggagetransfers.co.uk**

Walking holidays

Several companies offer complete walking packages including: accommodation, local information, maps, baggage transfer and transport.

Clwydian Walking Holidays 01291 689774 | **www.celtic-trails.com** | info@ celtic-trails.com

Train and buses

The North Wales coast has an excellent public transport network, which makes linear walks easy to organise. For public transport information across Wales, see Traveline Cymru. 0871 200 22 33 | **www.traveline-cymru.info**

North Wales Coast Line trains stop at Chester, Shotton, Flint, Prestayn, Rhyl, Pensarn, Colwyn Bay, Llandudno Junction (with links to Llandudno and Deganwy), Conwy, Penmaenmawr, Llanfairfechan and Bangor. Timetables from Arriva Trains Wales **www.arrivatrainswales.co.uk** or National Rail Enquiries **www.nationalrail.co.uk**. There are regular bus services along the coast run by a number of operators; Traveline Cymru will cover all operators but this website is also useful: **www.arrivabus.co.uk**

Taxis

Numerous taxi companies operate from all of the seaside resorts along the coast and there are far too many to mention. A few are listed here on the less touristy sections of the route where facilities are more limited but the list is not exhaustive. **Connah's Quay** A Class Cars, 01244 831218; AAA Cars 01244 830123 | **Flint** AtoB Cars, 01352 731000/734502; | **Talacre** RJ Cars, 07810 868972 | **Kimnel Bay** Abacus Taxis 01745 360054 | **Penmaenmawr** Starline Taxis, 01492 621171 | **Llanfairfechan** A5 Taxi 01248 360360

Cycle hire

Cycle path 5 runs along the North Wales Coast and much of the Coast path is ideal for cycling. Both these cycle hire companies are on the route

The Bike Hub, Rhyl, www.bikehubrhyl.uk, 01745 339758. They offer repairs and servicing as well as bike hire

Gogcog, Porth Eirias Colwyn Bay gogcogs.co.uk, 07423 010638

Boat Trips

Llandudno   Daily boat tours around the Great and Little Orme, April - October, 07961 561589

Llandudno Occasional steamer excursions call at Llandudno pier during the summer www.waverleyexcursions.co.uk, www.whitefunnel.co.uk

Conwy   Personalised tours along the Conwy Estuary|from Conwy Marina | **www.conwyboattours.co.uk**

Conwy Traditional sightseeing cruises from Conwy Quay, upriver into the Conwy Valley or downriver into Conwy Bay. 07917 343058 | **www.sightseeingcruises.co.uk**

Bangor Fast, comfortable passenger ribs operate from the Garth Jetty beside

Bangor Pier 01248 716335 info@bangorboattrips.com **www.bangorboat-trips.com**

Connah's Quay From Spring 2016 there will be regular boat trips in fully accessible boats along the River Dee from Connah's Quay Dock **www.qwa.org.uk**

Emergencies

In an emergency, call 999 or 112 and ask for the service your require: Ambulance, Police, Fire or Coastguard. North Wales police 01286 673347.

Tides

Short stretches of the Wales Coast Path and some alternative routes are only accessible on a low or outgoing tide. Check tide times before you go. Tide table booklets are widely available from TICs and local shops for around £1 or go online **www.tidetimes.org.uk** and choose your nearest location

Weather forecasts

For reliable, up-to-date weather forecasts, see **www.bbc.co.uk/weather** or **www.metoffice.gov.uk/weather/uk.**

Annual events

Connah's Quay River Festival: 2nd weekend in September
Flint Festival: Late June / early July
Prestatyn Walking Festival: Mid May www.prestatynwalkingfestival.co.uk
Numerous festivals and events throughout the year in Colwyn Bay, Conwy and Llandudno and are listed on **www.visitllandudno.org.uk**
Cerdedd Conwy run regular free guided walks throughout the year cerddedconwywalks.org

Further reading

Walks around Chester and the Dee Estuary, David Berry, Kittiwake Books.
ISBN 978-1-902-302-99-7

Walks around Llandudno and along the coast to Prestatyn, David Berry, Kittiwake Books.
ISBN 978-1-902-302-91-1

North Wales Pleasure Steamers, Andrew Gladwell, Amberwell.
ISBN 978-1-4456-0471-8

Conwy County Borough Council have produced a series of walks booklets covering the coastal area.
They can be downloaded from **www.conwy.gov.uk/walks**

Wales Coast Path: Official Guides

The **Official Guides** to the **Wales Coast Path** are endorsed by Natural Resources Wales, the Welsh government body which developed and manages the path. The guides break the Wales Coast Path into seven main sections, giving both long-distance and local walkers everything they need to enjoy all 870 miles of this world-class route.

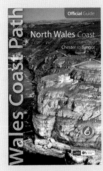

North Wales Coast
Chester to Bangor
ISBN: 978-0-9559625-1-6

Isle of Anglesey
Circuit from Menai Bridge
ISBN: 978-1-902512-15-0

Llŷn Peninsula
Bangor to Porthmadog
ISBN: 978-1-908632-24-1

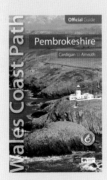

Pembrokeshire
Cardigan to Amroth
ISBN: 978-1-908632-23-4

**Carmarthen Bay &
Gower** *Tenby to Swansea*
ISBN: 978-1-908632-26-5

South Wales Coast
Swansea to Chepstow
ISBN: 978-1-908632-27-2

Wales Coast Path: Top 10 Walks

Award-winning pocket-size walking guides to the most popular, easy circular walks along key sections of the Wales Coast Path. The full series will cover the whole path in ten attractive guides.

Currently available

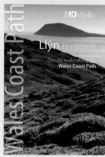

Top 10 Walks:
Llŷn Peninsula
ISBN: 978-1-902512-34-1

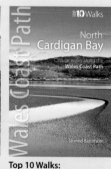

Top 10 Walks:
Cardigan Bay North
ISBN: 978-1-908632-13-5

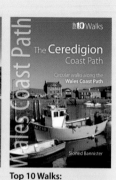

Top 10 Walks:
Ceredigion Caost
ISBN: 978-1-908632-28-9

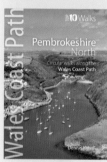

Top 10 Walks:
Pembrokeshire North
ISBN: 978-1-908632-29-6

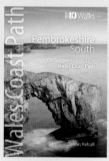

Top 10 Walks:
Pembrokeshire South
ISBN: 978-1-908632-30-2

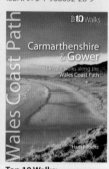

Top 10 Walks:
Carmarthenshire & Gower
ISBN: 978-1-908632-16-6

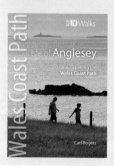

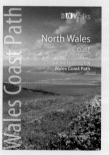

Available 2016

Top 10 Walks:
Isle of Anglesey

Top 10 Walks:
North Wales Coast

www.top10walks.co.uk
www.walescoastpath.co.uk